THE GREAT
HISPANIC HERITAGE

Frida Kahlo

THE GREAT HISPANIC HERITAGE

THE GREAT
HISPANIC HERITAGE

Frida Kahlo

John Morrison

CHELSEA HOUSE
PUBLISHERS
A Haights Cross Communications Company
Philadelphia

CHELSEA HOUSE PUBLISHERS

VP, NEW PRODUCT DEVELOPMENT Sally Cheney
DIRECTOR OF PRODUCTION Kim Shinners
CREATIVE MANAGER Takeshi Takahashi
MANUFACTURING MANAGER Diann Grasse

Staff for FRIDA KAHLO

ASSISTANT EDITOR Kate Sullivan
PRODUCTION EDITOR Jaimie Winkler
PHOTO EDITOR Sarah Bloom
SERIES & COVER DESIGNER Terry Mallon
LAYOUT 21st Century Publishing and Communications, Inc.

A Haights Cross Communications ⟋↖ Company

http://www.chelseahouse.com

First Printing

1 3 5 7 9 8 6 4 2

Library of Congress Cataloging-in-Publication Data

Morrison, John F., 1929–
    Frida Kahlo / John Morrison.
        p. cm.—(The Great Hispanic heritage)
Summary: A biography of the Mexican painter who survived a near-fatal bus accident
at the age of eighteen, learned to paint as a form of therapy, had a stormy marriage
with Diego Rivera, and became a world-famous artist. Includes bibliographical
references and index.
    ISBN 0-7910-7254-1 HC   0-7910 7517-6 PB
    1. Kahlo, Frida—Juvenile literature. 2. Painters—Mexico—Biography—Juvenile
literature. [1. Kahlo, Frida. 2. Artists. 3. Women—Biography.] I. Title. II. Series.
ND259.K33 M67 2002
759.972—dc21
                                                                2002152670

Table of Contents

1

The Unconquerable Spirit

Frida Kahlo nearly died that day, and the world would have been denied the pleasure and stimulation of viewing the dramatic and haunting paintings of one of Mexico's most heralded artists. In fact, it could be argued that the accident, as horrific as it was, made Frida the artist that she became. But at that moment on September 17, 1925, there was only pain and terror.

THE ACCIDENT

It was one of those flukes of fate that change a life forever. The bus was a new model, made of wood and brightly painted, with rows of seats facing each other. The 18-year-old schoolgirl and her boyfriend shouldn't have been on that bus that September day in 1925. They intended to take another bus for the ride to their home in Coyoacán, outside Mexico City. But Frida Kahlo discovered that a toy parasol that her friend, Alejandro Gómez Arias, had bought her during the day's shopping trip was missing.

In Kahlo's *retablo*, a small oil painting that commonly features saints to evoke protection, she depicts the horrifying streetcar accident that pierced her abdomen and left her permanently disfigured. The accident inflicted emotional wounds that lingered long after her physical wounds healed; Kahlo harnessed that pain to create some of the world's most haunting and emotional paintings.

The two retraced their steps, searching for the parasol. When they couldn't find it, they bought a balero, a cup and ball toy. Then they spotted the other bus and decided to take it home. In fact, they felt lucky that the vehicle came along when it did.

The bus driver made a critical mistake when he crossed at an intersection in the path of an electric streetcar. The trolley rammed the side of the bus and, for some reason, kept pushing the other vehicle until it was wedged against a wall. The heavier trolley continued to apply pressure on the bus until the wooden vehicle virtually exploded into splinters.

Frida's friend Alejandro was knocked unconscious and thrown out. When he came to, he was under the streetcar and his clothing had been shredded. The trolley was still moving, and he was sure he would be crushed. But the car finally stopped, and Alejandro was able to crawl out from under it. He hurried to the smashed bus to find Frida. He managed to work his way inside and was greeted by a horrifying sight. A metal handrail had rammed through Frida's body. Her clothing had been ripped away. She lay there naked, bleeding, and, strangely, covered with a fine coating of gold dust that a fellow passenger, a housepainter, had been carrying in a bag. A woman passenger thought she looked like a dancer and exclaimed, "Help for the little ballerina!"

Frida was so stunned that she didn't realize what had happened to her. She later wrote that her first thought was to look for the balero. "I did not assess the situation nor did I guess the kind of wounds I had," she wrote.

Alejandro started to pick Frida up to get her out of the wreckage, but she shrieked in pain. A man nearby said, "We have to take it out," speaking of the metal rod. He put a knee on her body and pulled the rod out of her. Alejandro said later that her screams were louder than the sirens of the ambulances that arrived. She was taken to the Red Cross Hospital and at first was placed among the more severely injured, whom the doctors thought could not be saved. But Alejandro pleaded with them to work on her, and she underwent the first of many operations she would endure for most of her painful life as medical science tried with little success to put her shattered body back together again.

Frida's spinal column was broken in three places in the lumbar region. Her collarbone and her third and fourth ribs were broken. Her right leg had 11 fractures, and her right foot was dislocated and crushed. Her left shoulder was out of joint, her pelvis broken in three places.

Frida always maintained that the metal rod that entered through her left hip exited through her vagina, damaging her uterus and rendering her incapable of bearing children. "I lost my virginity," she said. Alejandro said the wound was higher in the abdomen and maintained that Frida had invented the site of the exit, not uncharacteristic of her. She had a lifelong habit of embellishing experiences for dramatic effect.

Regardless, the accident had turned a high-spirited, happy schoolgirl, who loved to run and dance, to tease and joke, into a rigid, grim creature immobilized and enclosed in plaster casts and other devices and suffering constant pain.

"In this hospital," she told Alejandro, "death dances around my bed."

FRIDA BEGINS TO PAINT

As horrible as the accident was, it induced Frida to start painting as a form of therapy. Her mother rigged up a mirror on Frida's four-poster bed so she could paint while lying down. Although she had been drawing and sketching since childhood and had studied art and composition in school, it was during her convalescence (recovery) from the accident that she began seriously to try to put to canvas not only her personal visions, but the powerful feelings she had for the people and vistas of her native land.

Today, the work of Frida Kahlo is known around the world. In her short life—she died at 47—she produced some 200 paintings. Most were self-portraits, strong, vibrant pictures with colors as hot as the Mexican sun that she saw all around her in the people and the flora (plant life) and landscapes of Mexico, full of the passionate intensity of life that still surged throughout her broken body.

Actually, it took a long time for Frida to be recognized as an artist in her own right because for years she lived in the shadow of her husband, the great muralist, Diego Rivera.

During her lifetime, she deferred to him as the "master"—
master not only of their home, but also of the art they
each created.

Diego and Frida were certainly the odd couple of the art
world. His paintings were immense, typically covering entire
walls; hers were small, often no more that two feet square.
He was huge, over six feet tall, at times, weighing as much
as 300 pounds; she was petite, five feet three inches and rarely
weighing as much as 100 pounds. And, at 43, he was 19 years
older than she when they were married. Frida was darkly
attractive, given to colorful costumes and flamboyant jewelry
that drew all eyes to her on the street. Diego was drab and
homely, with a huge head, big, blubbery face, and bulging
eyes atop a bloated body.

Despite their differences, the couple shared a kind of
magnetism that drew others into their sphere. Both had
numerous romances, before and during their two marriages,
which caused raging battles and long separations. When the
fights and betrayals went beyond endurance, they divorced,
only to remarry a year later. It seemed they could neither live
with nor without each other.

During their heyday in the 1920s and 1930s, Frida Kahlo
and Diego Rivera met and mixed with some of the most
prominent people of their day: fellow artists, politicians,
movie stars, and the world's rich and famous. Their doings
were duly reported in the press of the day, and they were seen
as glamorous figures.

Both Kahlo and Rivera were dedicated to the principles
of the Mexican Revolution of 1910, and both celebrated the
revolutionary spirit in their art. Frida even tried to change
the date of her birth from 1907 to 1910, when leaders like
Emiliano Zapata, Pancho Villa, and Francisco Madero began
the struggle that would end the repressive 35-year regime of
Porfirio Díaz and transform the nation.

In a way, her afflictions paralleled those of her native land,
torn and troubled for centuries by foreign invaders, corrupt

officials, and brutal wars. But, like the spirit of Mexico, Kahlo's spirit was never seriously squelched. She might have been puzzled at how, years after her death, she has become something of a feminist icon. Women are inspired by the life of one of their sex who, though married to a strong, domineering man, still managed to do her own remarkable work and keep her independent spirit.

The pop singer Madonna, strongly individualistic and independent herself, owns two of Kahlo's paintings. Madonna said she identifies with Kahlo's "pain and her sadness." Exhibits of her work have been held around the world to great critical acclaim. In 2001, the U.S. Postal Service issued a 34-cent stamp of her 1933 *Self-portrait with a Necklace.* One of her paintings was in the Metropolitan Museum of Art's surrealism exhibit, although she probably would have objected to being classified as a surrealist.

A movie has been made of Frida Kahlo's life, starring Salma Hayek. Several books, including a novel, have been written about her. There has even been a traveling exhibit just of photographs of her. She was on the cover of *Time* magazine;

SURREALISM

Surrealism was an artistic and literary movement that began in the 1920s. The French poet André Breton is credited as its founder, but a number of French writers, such as Baudelaire, Rimbaud, and Apollinaire, also were involved in the movement's beginning. Those who practiced surrealism relied on dreams and the imagination to create their own reality. The movement was strongly influenced by the writings of psychiatrist Sigmund Freud, who wrote extensively about dreams and the mysteries of the unconscious mind.

Although even André Breton himself attempted to classify Kahlo as a surrealist, Kahlo disagreed, saying, "I never painted my dreams. I painted my own reality."

The U.S. Postal Service commemorated Kahlo's contribution to art with a stamp bearing her image in 2001. The first stamp honoring a Hispanic woman, it sealed Kahlo's status as a major presence for Mexicans and people of Hispanic descent everywhere.

Volvo used her image to sell cars to Hispanics. Her typically unsmiling, dark-browed visage can be found on posters, T-shirts, calendars, and many other objects in both the United States and Mexico. There have been Frida look-alike contests, Frida operas, plays, documentaries, even a cookbook. Frida Kahlo's former home in Coyoacán is now a museum and one of Mexico's hottest tourist attractions. Her paintings sell in the $10 million range.

What was there about this woman, crippled from the age of six by polio, smashed and broken in a horrendous street accident, not conventionally pretty, a heavy smoker and drinker, a dedicated Communist, abused and betrayed by both life and lovers, that has made her a heroine for many yearning souls, and a figure of almost mythic proportions?

It was not only her remarkable talent as a painter, her skill at producing art that resonates deeply in many people. There was also her indomitable spirit and love of life, characteristics that all the pain and disappointments she endured could not diminish. That spirit she carried to the end. In 1953, after her right leg had been amputated below the knee because of gangrene, she wrote in her diary: *"Pies para que los quiero, si tengo alas pa'volar?"* (Feet, why do I want them if I have wings to fly?)

One of her last paintings is a still life of ripe watermelons, inscribed with the words, *"Viva la vida"*—Long live life.

THE SERIOUS ONE

There she is in family photographs, the dark one, unsmiling, scowling at the camera. In some pictures, she is dressed in a man's suit, looking severe. Even photographed as a child, with a sister and a girlfriend in a formal studio setting, she is the serious one, while the other two radiate innocence. And yet, by all accounts, Frida Kahlo had a good childhood. Even after she was afflicted with polio at the age of six and left with a deformed right leg, she exhibited a spirit that was at times ungovernable.

Her father, Guillermo Kahlo, a German Jew of Hungarian descent, had a total of six daughters, including two by a previous marriage. But he was most fond of Frida, whom he called his *Liebe Frida* (Darling Frida). He pampered her greatly, especially after her bout with polio.

"Frida is my most intelligent daughter," he said. "She's most like me."

He was a photographer and, for a time, worked for the administration of President Porfirio Díaz, making good money. After Díaz was ousted by revolutionary forces in 1911, Guillermo had trouble making ends meet.

Frida's mother, Matilde Calderón, Guillermo's second wife, was part Indian. Her maternal grandfather was a Spanish general of Indian descent. She was a devout Catholic—to the point of bigotry—and this was a major factor in turning Frida against organized religion at an early age.

Frida was born Magdalena Carmen Frida Kahlo Calderón in the Casa Azul (Blue House) on Allende Street in the village of Coyoacán, a southern suburb of Mexico City, on July 6, 1907. Her father built the Casa Azul in 1904. It was a U-shaped building with an inner court filled with subtropical plants. Frida and Diego Rivera would live in the house for many years, and after her death, Diego would have it enlarged and turned into a museum dedicated to Frida's work and Mexican culture. Frida immortalized the house in a painting, *My Grandparents, My Parents and I,* in 1936. In it, she depicts herself as a naked little girl standing in the courtyard, holding ribbons that extend to images of her parents and their parents.

Frida's mother must have been a difficult woman. She refused to raise her husband's two daughters by his first marriage (his first wife died in childbirth) and had them sent to a convent orphanage. She was a sickly woman, especially after her last daughter, Cristina, was born just 11 months after Frida's birth, and she sought solace in the Catholic Church.

"My mother was excessively religious," Frida once said.

"We had grace before every meal and, while the others were concentrating on their inner selves, Christ and I would just look at one another and choke back our laughter."

When Frida contracted polio, she was confined to her bed for nine months and her right leg became withered, a deformity of which she was ashamed for the rest of her life. However, her doting father made her swim and ride a bicycle—sometimes to the point of exhaustion—to strengthen her limbs.

She was sent to a German elementary school, where schoolmates laughed at her withered leg and called her *Pata de Palo* (Wooden Leg). She became lonely and isolated. During this period, she created an imaginary playmate. She would blow on a window pane and draw a door on the foggy glass. She imagined herself going through the door, running across a plain to a building, which she entered to find her friend.

"I no longer remember her form and coloring, but I do know that she was a lot of fun and laughed a great deal, soundlessly, of course," she wrote years later. "She was very nimble and could dance."

Frida's life changed dramatically when her father decided to send her to the the Escuela Nacional Preparatoria (National Preparatory School), an excellent preparatory school in Mexico City, attended by the most privileged of the city's young. Her mother opposed the move because there were some 300 boys in the school and only a handful of girls. But Frida easily passed the entrance examination and entered an institution where her intellectual curiosity and interest in the arts would be satisfied. She decided that she eventually wanted to study medicine.

Frida was a rebellious teenager, setting her own style of dress, sometimes designing her own clothes, and often appearing in men's suits, her long black hair pulled back in a severe bun. She was attractive in an unusual way. Her dark eyebrows met in the middle, and she didn't bother to pluck them. She also had a faint mustache that she did not hesitate to include in her many self-portraits.

The penetrating eyes of the young, prep school-aged Kahlo denote the sharp mind of the woman she was to become. Kahlo was one of the only two young women in the Cachuchas, the rebellious prep school circle who devoted themselves to the cerebral pursuits of literature and socialist-nationalist ideas.

She defied convention from the start, but was fortunate to fall in with a band of intellectual and mischievous classmates at school who were also defying convention. They called themselves the Cachuchas, named after the jaunty caps they wore. This group, comprising seven boys and two girls, were both the pride and despair of the Preparatoria: pride because of their academic accomplishments, despair because of the mischief they liked to get into. In one of their pranks, they tied firecrackers to the tail of a dog, lit them, and sent the poor animal running through the corridors.

On another occasion, they decided to teach a lesson to a professor whom they considered boring. They detonated a firecracker above the podium where he was lecturing. The blast knocked out windows above the lectern, and glass showered the professor. However, he merely smoothed down his mussed hair, brushed the glass from his clothing, and went on with his boring lecture.

The Cachuchas disdained politics as beneath them, but they espoused a kind of romantic socialism combined with nationalism. They were influenced by the ideals of the Revolution and considered themselves disciples of José Vasconcelos, minister of public education under President Alvaro Obregón. Vasconcelos' aim was to make Mexican education truly Mexican, turning away from European influences. The Cachuchas heartily agreed with this philosophy. In addition to being rebels and mischief-makers, members of the Cachuchas reveled in being intellectually curious.

Being accepted by the Cachuchas was a great honor for Frida Kahlo. The members included boys, Frida and another girl, who would make names for themselves as adults, becoming professionals, educators, leaders of the nation, artists, and writers. They obviously liked Frida's intellectual curiosity, as well as her rebellious nature.

The leader of the group was Alejandro Gómez Arias, who was to be her first great love, and the friend who was with her on the fateful day of the streetcar accident. Arias would go on to become a highly regarded intellectual, lawyer, and political journalist.

Frida also enjoyed the company of other groups at the school. Among them was the Contemporaneos, an informal literary club, many of whose members would go on to make their mark in Mexican literature, politics, and the arts. Another group was the Maistros, a more radical band of free thinkers.

Still, her real pals were the Cachuchas, whose favorite hangout was the Ibero American Library, a short distance from the school. There they would argue, flirt, write papers, draw pictures and, most of all, read. They read everything. They devoured the works of many of the most famous authors of the world, Germans, Russians, French, English, Americans, and, of course, Mexican. Frida learned to read in three languages— Spanish, English, and German. Remembering her father's collection of philosophical treatises, she loved to discuss Hegel and Kant, among other great thinkers. She would call out the school window to Arias, "Alejandro, lend me your Spengler. I don't have anything to read on the bus." That no doubt would have been Oswald Spengler's *Decline of the West*, written by the German philosopher in 1918. Regrettably, the book was greatly admired by the Nazis.

The Cachuchas had competitions among themselves and their friends to find the best book and see who could read it first. They held dramatizations of what they read, attracting a wide and admiring audience.

One of Frida's few female friends was the other girl in the Cachuchas, Carmen Jaime, a very eccentric but interesting young lady who would grow up to become a scholar of seventeenth-century Spanish literature. She dressed in dark, masculine clothing and earned the nicknames "James" because of her manly attire and "Vampire" because she sometimes wore a black cape. Carmen was just the kind of person Frida, an eccentric herself, would find interesting. Carmen seemed to have read every philosophy book ever written, and their discussions would leave lesser minds in the dust.

Frida was able to earn high marks in school without putting in much effort. She had the enviable ability to read a text and easily remember its contents. She was presumptuous enough on occasion to urge the school's director to remove professors she found boring and ill informed. Needless to say, such behavior did not endear her to many of the teachers.

In 1922, Frida had her first encounter with Diego Rivera, who, along with several other artists, had been hired by Vasconcelos to paint a mural at the school that would reflect Mexican culture. The meeting was hardly promising. Frida teased him unmercifully and pulled tricks on him. He was 36 and soon to marry his mistress, Guadalupe "Lupe" Marín. Frida was only 15, but she told friends later, "My ambition is to have a baby by Diego Rivera."

Diego Rivera, Frida's Destiny

Diego Rivera might have been world famous when he began to paint a mural in Frida's National Preparatory School, the Prepartoria, but he didn't look the part. At 36, he was enormously fat, and he dressed like a slob. In those days, teachers and officials of the school were always properly dressed, the men often in homburg hats (felt hats with stiff, curled brims), black suits, and stiff collars. Rivera favored a floppy Stetson (broad-brimmed felt hat), baggy pants held up by a wide leather belt—sometimes a cartridge belt—and heavy black miner's boots. His wrinkled clothes looked as if he'd slept in them for a week. How could he help but be the subject of student fun at the hands of the mischievous Cachuchas and their most irreverent member, Frida Kahlo?

Rivera received a commission to paint the mural in the Bolivar Amphitheater, the school's auditorium. He was one of several artists hired by José Vasconcelos, the liberal minister of public education, to paint murals at the school as part of his continuing effort to bring truly Mexican art to the country.

Diego Rivera, already a famous painter, captured the attention of 15-year-old Kahlo when he was commissioned to paint a mural at the National Preparatory School (the Preparatoria), where Kahlo was a student. Rather than being repulsed by Rivera's slovenly dress and round belly, Kahlo found the robust artist fascinating.

It was Rivera's first mural. He called it *Creation*. It was a 1,000-square-foot work of art that was strongly influenced by European, especially Italian, styles, with a blend of early Mexican art. Rivera's model for Eve was his mistress, Lupe Marín, soon to be his wife. He painted her in the nude.

FRIDA'S TRICKS

The muralists at the Preparatoria, including Rivera, were frequently tormented by the students. The artists were like sitting ducks, high up on their scaffolds, more or less vulnerable to student pranks, despite the fact that students were banned from the amphitheater while the work was in progress. Sometimes the pranks caused serious damage. For instance, after a scaffold was built, there would be wood chips and shavings on the floor. The students would set these on fire, and sometimes the fire would badly damage the scaffolding and the work in progress. Some of the artists began carrying guns.

Because of his appearance and his habit of talking while working, Diego Rivera became an especially choice object of mischief, especially for Frida Kahlo, who took a particular pleasure in plaguing the artist with her tricks. Once she soaped the stairway that led to the amphitheater stage, where he was working on *Creation*. But Rivera, being the fat man that he was, always was careful where he walked and didn't slip on the soap. However, the same professor who was the subject of a student firecracker because of his boring lectures slipped on the soap and fell down the stairs.

Frida was intrigued by the beautiful models who accompanied Rivera on the scaffold to pose for him. Besides Lupe Marín, there was Nahui Olin, a well-known Mexican beauty. Frida delighted in using the presence of these models to tease Rivera. If Lupe was on the scaffold, Frida would shout to him, "Hey, Diego, here comes Nahui!" If Diego was alone on the scaffold and she saw Lupe arriving, she would call out, "Watch out, Diego, Lupe's coming!" as if he was up to no good and was about to be caught.

Frida obviously found Rivera fascinating, as did many women over the years. Of course, she was only 15, but no doubt more mature feelings were stirring within her. She once told a group of fellow students that her ambition was to have Rivera's baby, and said, "And I'm going to tell him so someday." The other students, especially the girls, were appalled. How could she be attracted to such a slovenly man, years older than she? Their reactions didn't bother Frida. "Diego is so gentle, so tender, so wise, so sweet," she said. "I'd bathe him and clean him."

Later, Frida remembered that even while she taunted him

and called him names, she was thinking to herself, "You'll see, *panzon* (fat belly), now you don't pay any attention to me, but one day I'll have a child by you." One of Frida's great tragedies, of course, was that, because of her accident, she couldn't have a child by anyone.

RIVERA TAKES NOTICE OF YOUNG FRIDA

Rivera recalled being amused by the impish little girl who came to visit him while he was working. In his autobiography, *My Art, My Life,* he recalled seeing Frida one day burst through the auditorium door and come striding up to where he was working and where Lupe was quietly knitting.

"She was dressed like any other high school student, but her manner immediately set her apart," he wrote. "She had unusual dignity and self-assurance, and there was a strange fire in her eyes." She asked permission to watch him work, and he said he would be charmed. Lupe, however, began to be jealous and started to insult the girl. Frida paid no attention, and Lupe herself was intrigued. "Look at that girl! Small as she is, she does not fear a tall, strong woman like me," Diego quoted her as saying. "I like her."

By the time Frida first encountered Rivera in 1922, he was a well-known artist whose work was in galleries and private hands around the world. He had studied in Spain and Paris, where he became friends with such renowned artists as Pablo Picasso and Amadeo Modigliani. His years abroad saw many dramatic upheavals in the world—World War I, which changed Europe forever; the Russian Revolution, led by Vladimir Ilych Lenin and Leon Trotsky, who would one day go to Mexico and have a profound impact on both Diego and Frida. In Rivera's native Mexico, he saw long years of violent change in both government and society after the Revolution of 1910.

YOUNG RIVERA

Rivera was born on December 8, 1886, in Guanajuato, an old mining city in the Sierra Madres, 170 miles northwest of Mexico City. He was fortunate to have a father, also named Diego Rivera, who encouraged his early interest in art. He studied art at the Academy of San Carlos and began to sell his paintings while still a teenager.

In 1906, his father showed some of his work to the governor of Veracruz, Teodoro Dehesa, who was greatly impressed. Dehesa offered to give the young artist a monthly allowance to study in Europe. Diego, then 20, earned money for the passage to Spain by selling his work at two exhibits. It was thus that his European experience began. While in Europe, Diego had many romances. People—both men and women—were attracted to this robust, outgoing, intelligent and well-read "cowboy" from Mexico. In Paris, he lived with a Russian artist named Angeline Beloff, who bore him a son, Diego Jr., who died before he reached two years of age. But the artist also met and wooed several women. Frida was not to be even among his first.

In 1910, Rivera returned to Mexico for the centennial celebration of Mexico's independence from Spain. He would show his work at his old school, the Academy of San Carlos. The day the exhibit opened, November 20, 1910, Francisco Madero called for a general uprising against the dictatorial rule of Porfirio Díaz, the beginning of the Mexican Revolution—today, a national holiday.

Revolutionary forces were winning battles against Díaz's army. In the north, Francisco "Pancho" Villa and Alvaro Obregón, future president of Mexico, were the revolutionary heroes, while in the south, Emiliano Zapata commanded a large following.

In honor of the Revolution, Rivera designed a poster showing a family plowing a field while an image of Jesus looked down on them. The poster read, "The Distribution of Land to the Poor Is Not Contrary to the Teachings of Our Lord Jesus Christ and the Holy Mother Church." It was mass-produced and widely distributed. Rivera also visited Zapata in the state of Morelos and was impressed by the communes that the legendary leader had set up to work the land. Working together without bosses, the farmers produced sugar on a large scale for eight years. Rivera painted a portrait of Zapata, who was killed in an ambush on April 10, 1919.

CUBISM

Rivera experimented with Cubism, an art form in which figures were depicted as fragmented objects in space. Picasso and Georges Braque were behind the Cubist movement. Rivera plunged into it with his usual ferocious energy and produced about 200 Cubist paintings. He became an important part of the Cubist movement. Working at a fast pace, he would produce as many as five paintings a month in this style. Through Picasso's influence, he was given a one-man show at Paris' Galerie Weill in April 1914. Despite his success with Cubism, Rivera gradually became disillusioned with this art form when he realized, as he put it, "all this innovation had little to do with real life." He decided that the work of Picasso and the other Cubists was for the wealthy. Rivera wanted to paint for the people.

By this time, an allowance Rivera had been receiving from the government of Francisco Madero was cut off when Madero was assassinated in 1913. And just two months after Rivera's one-man show, the Archduke Francis Ferdinand of Austria was shot and killed, an event that would lead to World War I.

After a brief sojourn on the island of Majorca, Rivera and

THE MEXICAN REVOLUTION

A movie was made about the life of Emiliano Zapata, the Mexican revolutionary, in 1952. *Viva Zapata!* starred Marlon Brando and Anthony Quinn. Several movies were made about Francisco "Pancho" Villa. He was a much more colorful figure. Zapata operated in the south from the state of Morelos, and Villa operated in the north. They were leaders of the revolution of 1910 that led to the overthrowing of Porfirio Díaz after 35 years of tyrannical rule. Villa was an uncontrollable character, and he even invaded the United States, staging a raid on Columbus, New Mexico. President Woodrow Wilson sent General John J. "Black Jack" Pershing to find Villa, but he failed. Pershing later led American forces in World War I.

Angeline returned to Paris to find a nation at war. Times were tough for everyone, and Diego and Angeline had trouble making ends meet. Millions of men and women were being slaughtered in that brutal war, and nobody was in the mood to buy art. Rivera met the French artist Henri Matisse and the revolutionary Russian writer Ilya Ehrenburg. He had a fling with a Russian artist, Marvena Vorobev-Stebelska, but, after living with her for a short time, returned to Angeline. Such behavior was typical of the way Rivera dealt with women through most of his life, finding stable relationships but always veering off to play with a more exciting lady, then returning to stability.

Events were multiplying in Europe. French soldiers, sick of war, staged a mutiny. The United States declared war on Germany. And, in Russia, Leon Trotsky led thousands of workers in a successful insurrection, taking over Moscow. It was October 25, 1917, the start of the Russian Revolution, which would have such a profound effect on the entire world.

Rivera and his Russian friends were excited. Lenin promised to give the peasants land and put the workers in charge of industry. That was the Communist ideal. On March 3, 1918, Trotsky signed a separate peace with Germany. But World War I ended eight months later, November 11, 1918, when Germany agreed to an armistice with all of its enemies.

While still living in Paris, Rivera met the muralist David Alfaro Siqueiros, who also went to the Academy of San Carlos. Siqueiros was now 21, and he and Rivera became close friends. Siqueiros had fought with the armies of Alvaro Obregón and had attained the rank of captain. He regaled Rivera with stories of the Mexican Revolution, in which 2 million people had died.

RETURN TO MEXICO

Rivera began to realize that he had to return to Mexico. Obregón was elected president in 1920, and Rivera believed the time was ripe for a new era of Mexican art. After a 17-month tour of Italy studying Renaissance art, he left Angeline Beloff in June and returned to his native land. He came to realize how badly he had

Alvaro Obregón was one of many rebels involved in the Mexican Revolution that began in 1910. After the dictator Porfirio Díaz was overthrown, Obregón was elected the second president of Mexico in 1920. It was under Obregón's administration that Rivera was commissioned to paint the mural at the Preparatoria, where he would meet his future wife, Kahlo, for the first time.

treated Beloff. "She gave me everything a good woman can give to a man," he later wrote. "In return, she received from me all the heartache and misery that a man can inflict upon a woman." Beloff lived alone for the rest of her life. Rivera never returned to her.

When he arrived in Mexico, Rivera was greeted by José Vasconcelos, Obregón's minister of public education, who asked him to do a mural at the National Preparatory School, where the mischievous young Frida Kahlo was a star student.

3

Sundays with the "Little Devil"

Alejandro Gómez Arias was the "big man on campus" at the Preparatoria. Handsome and smart, he was the center of attention among the cliques of bright young students who were destined to find important roles for themselves as adults. He was adept at conversation, whether discussing literature, philosophy, art or just school gossip. Fellow students tended to hang on his every word. Arias also was very nationalistic. He urged his friends to dedicate themselves to the "great destiny" of Mexico. Kahlo was attracted to him, as she was always attracted to the star of the show, to the great and near-great, who always seemed to cluster about her. Arias remembered her as having a "childlike manner, but at the same time she was quick and dramatic in her urge to discover life."

He was several classes ahead of Kahlo, which seemed to add to his attractiveness. She always gravitated toward older, more experienced, and worldly men. Not that Arias was a man in those days, but he was obviously on his way to being an important one some day. Kahlo wrote

Kahlo's first love, Alejandro Gómez Arias, speaks to the Congreso de Mérida. Arias stole Kahlo's heart with his magnetic personality and the passionate rhetoric that would later benefit his political life. It was for Arias that Kahlo painted her first self-portrait, a gift she hoped would persuade him to return to her, despite her infidelities with other men.

many letters to him, many of which were accompanied by drawings. "You can see what progress I am making in drawing," she wrote. "Now you know that I am a prodigy in matters of art." It was during the summer of 1923 that their relationship deepened into love. She began to refer to Arias as her fiancé.

On November 30, 1923, there was a rebellion against President Obregón that brought fighting to Mexico City. Vasconcelos resigned during the fighting, but returned to his job briefly after the insurrection was put down (with 7,000 dead). But he quit again when Plutarco Elías Calles became president. To protest his resignation, students at the Preparatoria took out their anger on the murals in the school, scratching curses into the plaster and spitting on them. Kahlo didn't take part in any of these demonstrations. Her parents kept her at home.

Kahlo's letters to Arias were full of love and yearning, as if she had a premonition that their relationship was doomed. Her passionate letters to him continued while she was recovering from the streetcar accident on September 17, 1925, which put her in the hospital for a month and then kept her confined to her home in Coyoacán.

On December 18, three months after the accident, Kahlo was well enough to visit Mexico City. Since she had missed her final examinations at the Preparatoria, she did not go back to the school. Her family needed money and she went to work. She helped her father in his photographic studio and took other part-time jobs. Frida and Alejandro were drifting farther apart. He apparently accused her of having affairs with other men, which she admitted.

"Although I have said, 'I love you' to many, and I have had dates with and kissed others, underneath it all I never loved anyone but you," she wrote to Alejandro in December 1925.

It was while trying to bring Alejandro back to her that she painted her first self-portrait. She started it in the summer of 1926, when she became ill and had to be confined to her home. She finished it the next September. Unlike many of her later self-portraits, this one is a more formal pose, and she made herself look elegant, garbed in a wine-red velvet dress with an elegant brocade collar and looking quite beautiful. Like several of her later self-portraits, it was a gift to a man whom she was begging to love her. On the back she wrote, "Frieda Kahlo at 17 years of age in September 1926. Coyoacán." Beneath it were the German words, *Heute ist Immer Noch* (today still goes on.)

Frida sometimes spelled her name Frieda. And she actually was 19, a falsehood stemming from her lifelong habit of subtracting two or three years from her age so she seemed to have been born in 1910, at the outbreak of the Mexican Revolution, not her real birth year of 1907.

FRIDA'S RECOVERY

From the time of her accident, Frida was in almost constant pain, and she had numerous relapses that put her back in the hospital. She began her self-portrait after doctors found that three of her vertebrae were out of place and she had to be placed in casts again. She turned to painting as a way to overcome her boredom and loneliness. She used oil paints and brushes that her father, an amateur artist, kept in his studio. Her first subjects— besides herself—were friends she had known in school.

In letters to Alejandro in this period, she describes her pain: "I'm fed up with so much sickness, like an old woman, I don't know how I'll be when I'm 30, you'll have to carry me all day wrapped in cotton. . . ." But Alejandro left for Germany and was gone for several months. There is some speculation that his parents sent him to Europe to cool off his relationship with Frida, of whom they didn't approve. Her letters to him continued to describe her loneliness and pain, and she begged him to love her. But Frida and Alejandro drifted further and further apart. Alejandro was kept busy with his university studies, and Frida with her art.

A year after Frida's accident she asked Alejandro why he was studying so much. She wondered what he expected to learn about life. She described her own lost hope of finding anything behind the emptiness of daily experience:

> A little while ago, not much more than a few days ago, I was a child who went about in a world of colors, of hard and tangible forms. Everything was mysterious and something was hidden. Guessing what it was was a game for me.
>
> If you knew how terrible it is to know suddenly, as if a bolt of lightning elucidated the earth. Now I live in a painful planet, transparent as ice, but it is as if I had learned everything at once in seconds. My friends, my companions became women slowly, I became old in instants and everything today is bland and lucid. I know that nothing lies behind. If there was something, I would see it. . . .

Even so, Frida's inner spirit refused to give in. Despite her pain, she was an inspiration to her friends. One of them, Aurora Reyes, remembered that Frida "always acted happy, she gave her heart.

She had an incredible richness, and though one went to see her to console her, one came away consoled." Another friend, Adelina Reyes, said, "When we went to visit her when she was sick, she played, she laughed, she commented, she made caustic criticisms, witticisms, and wise opinions. If she cried, no one knew it."

FRIDA REENTERS LIFE
Late in 1927, Frida had recuperated enough to resume something of a normal life. At that time, many of her old friends from the Preparatoria, including Alejandro, were involved in Mexican politics, which frequently turned violent. Frida became friendly with a young student demonstrator named German de Campo. He was a fiery speaker who was always elegantly dressed, usually with a flower in his buttonhole, and sporting a cane. It was De Campo who introduced Frida to his friend, Tina Modotti. Modotti was an Italian-born American photographer, very beautiful and very independent. She had come to Mexico with her lover, a famous photographer named Edward Weston. When Weston returned to the United States, she stayed on in Mexico.

Frida Kahlo soon became involved with the artists, writers, and political activists who had gathered around the revolutionary Cuban Communist Julio Antonio Mella. Mella and Alejandro Gómez Arias were law students together. They were both opposed to the government of Plutarco Elías Calles, president of Mexico from 1924 to 1928. But Arias didn't approve of many of the radicals in this group and was not really a part of it. This was another factor that led to the eventual end of his relationship with Kahlo. Unlike her former boyfriend, Kahlo was strongly attracted to these people—and to the Communist Party.

REACQUAINTANCE WITH DIEGO RIVERA
Death and violence were part of the life of Mexico in those days. German de Campo was murdered by agents of Calles for his anti-government speeches. And on January 10, 1929, Mella was shot down by a Cuban gunman while walking on a Mexico City street with Modotti.

President of Mexico from 1924 to 1928, Plutarco Elías Calles aroused disdain in both Kahlo's group of friends and Arias. Despite their mutual disapproval of Calles, Kahlo and Arias would ultimately end their relationship.

Kahlo and Modotti became good friends. Kahlo admired the older woman's spirit and energy. She began to attend parties and meetings of the artists and political activists, many of whom were either Communists or had strong Communist leanings. Among the artists who attended these get-togethers were the muralists, Orozco, Siqueiros and, of course, Diego Rivera. It's generally believed that Kahlo became reacquainted with Rivera at these parties. Rivera had joined the Communist

Party in 1922, and he had contributed artwork to the cause. He also gave rousing speeches to workers. Some called him the "Lenin of Mexico."

The story is told that he impressed Kahlo by shooting a phonograph with a pistol at one of the parties. In her own account, Kahlo said everybody was carrying pistols in those days, shooting out street lamps and taking pot shots at signs and anything else that showed itself as a likely target in the streets. And she recalled being impressed when Rivera shot the phonograph. However, this was not the incident that got them together again. She said she took four pictures to him while he was painting a mural at the Ministry of Public Education and asked him to look at them.

"Without hesitating a moment, I said to him, 'Diego, come down,'" she wrote, "and so, since he is so humble, so agreeable, he came down. 'Look, I didn't come to flirt with you or anything, even though you are a womanizer, I came to show you my painting. If it interests you, tell me so, if it doesn't interest you, tell me that too, so I can get to work on something else to help my parents.'"

SENATOR JOSEPH R. McCARTHY

In the 1950s, there were strong anti-Communist feelings in the United States, partly brought on by the Cold War and fears of Soviet expansion. A Republican U.S. senator named Joseph R. McCarthy of Wisconsin took advantage of this fear to win political power. He claimed he had a list of Communists in the State Department. He never produced the list, but many people believed him. He was chairman of a Senate investigations committee in 1952 and held hearings to root out Communist influence in the government. The hearings were televised and millions watched. Careers were ruined by his accusations. He finally went too far by accusing high government officials, and he was censured (formally criticized) by the Senate. He lost power and died in 1957 at the age of 49.

Rivera said he liked her work, especially the self-portrait she showed him. The other three, he told her, were too much influenced by other artists. He asked her to paint another picture and he would come to her home on Sunday. He did, and he told her she was talented. That visit to the Casa Azul in Coyoacán was the beginning of Rivera's courtship of Frida Kahlo. From then on, he came every Sunday for a visit.

One day, Kahlo's father, Guillermo, took Rivera aside and said, "I've got the feeling that you're interested in my daughter, is that so?"

"I certainly am," Rivera replied, "otherwise I wouldn't come all the way to Coyoacán so often."

"Do you realize she's a little devil?" Guillermo asked him.

"I know," Rivera said.

"All right, you've been warned," Guillermo said.

It's not known exactly when it dawned on Rivera that this young lady (she was 21; he was 41) was the impish little girl who had tormented him back in 1922 when he was painting at her school.

Kahlo had once said she suffered two serious accidents in her life. One was the streetcar crash that crippled her for life and the second was meeting Diego Rivera. Her life with this strong man and her determination to emerge from his shadow and earn recognition for her artistic talent were about to begin.

The Elephant and the Dove

MARRIAGE TO DIEGO RIVERA

Frida Kahlo and Diego Rivera were married on August 21, 1929, in Frida's hometown of Coyoacán. The wedding was a civil ceremony, the only kind recognized in Mexico after the Revolution. Frida and Diego had fallen in love rather quickly after Diego had begun visiting her to talk about her painting. Rivera was later to say that Frida became "the most important thing in my life." Unfortunately, he didn't always show it by his behavior.

By this time, Rivera had had many relationships with women, including a church marriage to Lupe Marín, which wasn't considered legal. He had a son by his Russian mistress, Angeline Beloff, and a daughter by the Russian artist Marevna Vorobev-Stebelska. His son died before reaching age 2, and Rivera didn't acknowledge his daughter as being his own for many years. These incidents were only the beginning of Rivera's messy relationships with women. However, he seemed to sincerely love Kahlo, and despite having many affairs with

36

Kahlo and Rivera pose in 1931, shortly after their marriage. Though few of Kahlo's friends could understand her attraction to the large, homely Rivera, it was Kahlo's adolescent wish to be Rivera's wife. The union also proved beneficial for Kahlo's family, whom Rivera assisted financially.

other women during their marriage, loved her until her death.

Kahlo's religious mother refused to attend the ceremony in the Coyoacán town hall because it was a civil ceremony, but her father was there. Guillermo Kahlo gave Rivera another piece of advice before the ceremony began.

"Now, look, my daughter is a sick person and all her life she's going to be sick," he said. "She's intelligent but not pretty. Think it over if you like, and if you still wish to marry her, marry her, I give you my permission."

Kahlo, whose style of dress changed frequently over the years, depending on her mood and her political views, had to borrow clothes for the wedding. She borrowed a skirt, blouse and *rebozo,* a Mexican stole, from her maid. The wedding day turned out to be a poor start to a marriage. First of all, Rivera's former wife, Lupe Marín, showed up and made a scene. She compared her physical attributes with Frida's, describing her own as more attractive, and stormed out. Then Rivera proceeded to get very drunk at the wedding party at the home of Roberto Montenegro. He fired his pistol, scaring the guests, broke a man's finger, and destroyed some furnishings. Frida and Diego got into a fight, and she ran away in tears. They didn't get together again for several days.

Despite the shaky start, their marriage made the society columns of newspapers around the world. Diego Rivera was famous, even though his wife was not well known at the time. When photographer Tina Modotti wrote to Edward Weston in September 1929 to tell him about the wedding, she didn't even mention Frida Kahlo by name, but just referred to her as a "lovely nineteen-year-old girl, of German father and Mexican mother, a painter herself." Then she added in Spanish, "*A ver que sale.*" (Let's see how it works.)

Kahlo's friends were shocked that she would take as her husband this fat, homely *old* man. They considered the union *una cosa monstruosa* (a hideous thing). Many said the union was like a marriage between an elephant and a dove. But for Kahlo's parents, ill and in bad financial straits, things worked out quite well. Rivera went on to pay off their mortgage and help them in other ways. As for Kahlo, marriage to the famous artist meant she could travel in Mexican, American, and European artistic and intellectual circles. She enjoyed the attention she received as the wife of Diego Rivera, although she would soon be eager to be recognized as an artist in her own right.

CHANGING STYLE OF DRESS AND ART

It's interesting to notice how Frida's manner of dress reflected the changing conditions of her life. In her teenage years, she had sometimes worn men's clothing. After her first introduction to the Communist Party, a political party that does not believe in private ownership, she took to wearing the plain red shirt of the party, with her hair cut short and pulled tightly back. In fact, a painting by Rivera, *Ballad of the Revolution*, in 1928 shows her in this severe costume, the red star of Communism on her shirt, passing out guns to workers.

But after their marriage, Rivera encouraged Kahlo to adopt the colorful Mexican-Indian costumes worn by the women of the Isthmus of Tehuantepec. For most of the rest of her life, Kahlo dressed in the Tehuana Indian manner, with flowing skirts and dramatic jewelry of silver and jade. She wore her hair swept up and decorated with ribbons, flowers, and combs. She frequently painted self-portraits of herself in those exotic costumes, and she certainly attracted attention on the streets, not only of Mexico City, but of cities in the United States and Europe. One observer said she made herself into a work of art.

Some critics have said Rivera also influenced Kahlo's art. They point to *The Bus*, an almost mural-like painting done in 1929 of people sitting in a row on a bus. Not only is Rivera's muralistic style there, but also his political views. A well-dressed man holding a bag of coins represents capitalism. Seated next to him is a pretty woman who might be his "trophy" wife, or his girlfriend. The other figures include a barefoot peasant woman, a worker holding a wrench, a housewife with a market basket, and a boy looking out of the window. Unlike Rivera's sweeping wall-sized murals, however, *The Bus* is only 10¼ by 22 inches.

Among Kahlo's other notable paintings of this period was *Portrait of Virginia (Niña)*, depicting a lovely little girl who, interestingly enough, has Kahlo's famous eyebrows. An unusual touch is that her dress is held together by a safety pin. Another work of that period is an amazing portrait of the agriculturist Luther Burbank. It shows him as half-man, half-vegetable, rising out of his own corpse. This painting, done in 1931, is considered by critics to represent a turning point in Kahlo's art career. From then on, she would follow her own vision of reality.

It has to be said, too, that Rivera encouraged his wife to go her own way in art, not to copy him or any other artist. And there was never any hint that he was jealous of her accomplishments.

SETTING UP THEIR HOME

After the wild wedding day and a brief, angry separation, the couple moved into Rivera's house on the first block of Avenida Reforma in Mexico City. "For furniture, we had a narrow bed, a dining set that Frances Toor gave us, with a long black table, and a little yellow kitchen table that my mother gave us," Kahlo said in an interview. (Toor was editor of *Mexican Folkways* magazine.) She said the table was used for Rivera's extensive collection of archaeological specimens. He was an avid collector of pieces of Mexican history he encountered on his travels around the country.

Kahlo was a devoted wife, and she was upset when she discovered she wasn't able to have Rivera's baby. She had an abortion after three months of pregnancy when it was learned the fetus was in the wrong position.

"I cried inconsolably," she said. "But I distracted myself fixing meals, cleaning house, painting at times, and going along with Diego each day to the scaffolds."

By this time, Rivera was working on a commission to decorate the stairwell at the National Palace in Mexico City with murals. It was to be a narrative history of Mexico, and he was to work on these murals into the 1940s. They illustrate in dramatic figures and blazing colors the country's history from before the Spanish conquest into the turmoil of the 1920s and 1930s. The way he shows the struggle of the Mexican people against their oppressors strongly reflects his Communist leanings, but no one seemed to mind. Much later in New York City, someone did mind—and the fight between Rivera and

Rivera was commissioned to paint the stairwells of Mexico City's National Palace with patriotic murals. His success as an artist in Mexico spread across the border, and he was later asked to contribute his talents in the United States. In this photo, Rivera paints a mural illustrating California's contributions to the nation. The woman depicted in the mural represents California, and in her hands she holds figures and emblems symbolizing this western state's products and activities.

Nelson Rockefeller would become the stuff of legend.

Meanwhile, Kahlo was playing the dutiful housewife. She visited her husband on the scaffolds, taking him his lunch and commenting on his work. "He really liked me to come along bringing his lunch in a basket covered with flowers," she said. Rivera's former wife, Lupe Marín, had put that idea into Kahlo's head. After the scene at the wedding, Lupe became Kahlo's good friend and even helped her furnish their house.

Rivera also enjoyed having his wife comment on his painting and often took her criticism to heart.

FRIDA SPARKLES

One of the key figures in Rivera's mural was Emiliano Zapata, the Mexican revolutionary from the state of Morelos. The artist depicted Zapata as leading a white horse. In actuality, Zapata's horse was black, and Kahlo pointed out this discrepancy. "Diego, how can you paint Zapata's horse white?" she demanded. He gave her a lame excuse, basically that he thought it looked better white, and the horse remained that color. However, when she complained that the horse's legs were too thick, he handed over his paint brush and let her repaint the animal's legs.

Kahlo's personality at that time was described by her friend, Luis Cardoza y Aragón: "Frida was what she always was, a marvelous woman. There was a spark in her that was growing and beginning to light up her canvases, to light up her life and, in turn, the lives of others." It's interesting that so many of her friends described how they felt better by simply being in her presence.

RIVERA'S POLITICAL AND DOMESTIC TROUBLES

Rivera got in trouble with his Communist comrades by accepting commissions from the Mexican government, associating with capitalists, and accepting their money. This was to be a lifelong conflict between Rivera's opposition to capitalism and his eagerness to take capitalists' money so he could paint the murals that he felt needed to be painted.

He was finally kicked out of the party. But in typical Rivera fashion, he turned his expulsion into theater. He went to a party convention in 1929 armed with what looked like a pistol concealed under a handkerchief. By this time, he held a high position in the party. He sat down and launched into a speech:

> I, Diego Rivera, general secretary of the Communist Party of
> Mexico, accuse the painter Diego Rivera of collaboration with
> the petty bourgeois Mexican government. He accepted a
> commission to decorate the stairwell of the National Palace.
> This contravenes the interests of the Comintern. Therefore,
> the painter Diego Rivera must be expelled from the Com-
> munist Party by the general secretary, Diego Rivera.

He then stood up and exposed the "pistol." He smashed it into pieces and walked out. The pistol was made of clay. (*Bourgeois* is French for the middle class, but it carries a negative meaning. *Comintern* refers to the first congress of the Communist Party in 1919, formed to take control of the Communist movement throughout the world. *Contravene* means to act in opposition to something.)

Despite his flippant behavior, Rivera was deeply hurt by his expulsion from the Communist Party, because he felt he remained loyal to its principles. Kahlo, who had joined the party in 1928, quit in solidarity with her husband.

While Kahlo was suffering through her abortion, she learned that Rivera was having an affair with one of his assistants. These were two serious blows to her—one, that she probably could never have a child, and two, that she could never trust Rivera to be faithful to her. Kahlo was either going to have to live with his infidelities or get away from him entirely. She would always be torn by these two unsatisfactory choices.

In the fall of 1930, she and Rivera left Mexico for their first visit to the United States. It would be another important milestone in Kahlo's life, with experiences both high and low.

COMING TO THE UNITED STATES

When Frida Kahlo and Diego Rivera arrived in San Francisco in November 1930, they found a country in the throes of the Great Depression. The stock market had crashed in October 1929 and sent the economy reeling. Unemployment was over 20 percent, and there were bread and soup lines in San Francisco when the Riveras arrived.

The couple was not directly affected by the crumpled economy. Rivera had commissions to paint murals in the San Francisco Stock Exchange and the California School of Fine Arts, which later became the San Francisco Art Institute. Although he liked to say he arrived in the United States as a "spy" to spread his revolutionary ideas, Rivera actually was fascinated by the achievements of capitalism, particularly heavy industry and the machinery that made it run. He loved to include in his paintings massive machines and the strong men who worked them. Rivera once said, "Perhaps future generations will recognize the machine as the art of our day."

The rich business people who hired Rivera didn't seem to mind that he was a devoted Communist, the "Lenin of Mexico." They didn't seem to care that he showed images of the great industrialists, John D. Rockefeller, Jr., Henry Ford, and J.P. Morgan, as grotesque caricatures in his paintings or that he

THE GREAT DEPRESSION

Wild speculation in the stock market was a contributing factor to the Great Depression of the 1930s in the United States. More and more people were investing in stocks in the late 1920s, driving up stock prices; they were often borrowing money to buy more stock. This caused the market to crash in October 1929. People lost their savings and businesses failed. The next 10 years were called the Great Depression. Unemployment was more than 20 percent. Men who were once businessmen sold apples in the street to make money, and people were lined up for soup at charity kitchens. President Franklin D. Roosevelt started many programs to help people find jobs, but it wasn't until the United States entered World War II that war production put people back to work and revitalized the dragging American economy.

filled his murals with the hammer-and-sickle symbol of Communism and pictures of Communist leaders. It wasn't until his run-in with John D. Rockefeller, Jr.'s son, Nelson Rockefeller, that Rivera's ideas were seriously challenged.

Actually, Rivera's behavior at this time angered the Communists more than it did the capitalists. He was criticized as being the "painter for millionaires" and for consorting with the Mexican government, now controlled by the reactionary Calles administration.

In Mexico, Communists, their sympathizers, and even union supporters were frequently arrested, deported, or simply made to vanish. But Rivera managed to charm Calles' education minister, José Manuel Puig Casauranc, who called Rivera the "philosopher of the brush," and he was kept on the government payroll. Rivera was a master of what is now known as "networking." He made connections with friends and supporters all over the world, who helped him obtain commissions and show his work to the public, just as sculptor Ralph Stackpole helped him to get the San Francisco commissions.

When Kahlo and Rivera arrived in San Francisco, they moved into Stackpole's large studio on Montgomery Street in the city's art neighborhood. One of their neighbors, Lucille Blanch, an artist whose husband, Arnold Blanch, was teaching at the California School of Fine Arts, remembered Kahlo as being shy about her own work.

"Frida did not set herself up as an artist," Lucille said. "We were both painters yet we did not talk about art. She scintillated in her talk, made fun of everything and everybody, laughing at things sportively and perhaps snobbishly. She was very critical if she thought something was pretentious, and often laughed at San Franciscans."

Kahlo and Rivera were well covered by the press. They were news, although the reporters pretty much ignored Kahlo. They concentrated on Rivera, the controversial "wild man" from Mexico, who had come to shake up the American art scene.

Rivera became fascinated with the female tennis star, Helen

Kahlo continued to develop her painting skills in the early years of her marriage, but she remained shy about her work. Though Kahlo deferred to Rivera as the better artist at first, she would later grow to recognize the genius behind her own work, which Rivera would praise as being among "the most powerful and truthful human documents of our times."

Wills, and used her as a model in some of his paintings. While he was busy with his murals, Kahlo toured San Francisco. She was especially intrigued by Chinatown, and she wrote to a friend that the Chinese children were so beautiful. "Yes, they are really extraordinary. I would love to steal one so that you could see for yourself."

However, she was not altogether happy among Americans. "I do not like the gringo people," she wrote. "They are boring and they all have faces like unbaked rolls (especially the old women)."

Kahlo met the photographer Edward Weston, Tina Modotti's former lover, and he described her as "a little doll alongside Diego, but a doll in size only, for she is strong and quite beautiful, shows very little of her father's German blood. Dressed in native costume, even to huaraches (sandals), she causes much excitement on the streets of San Francisco. People stop in their tracks to look in wonder."

It was in San Francisco that Kahlo met Dr. Leo Eloesser, a well-known physician who specialized in bone surgery. While in San Francisco, Frida was hospitalized for a problem with her foot and Dr. Eloesser took care of her. He became a lifelong friend and medical adviser.

After a brief return to Mexico, Kahlo and Rivera returned to San Francisco, where Rivera began the mural for the California School of Fine Arts. Entitled *The Making of a Fresco,* it shows Rivera seated on a scaffold, his back to the viewer, painting a mural of a helmeted worker at the controls of a machine. Also in the painting are school officials and the school architect, Arthur Brown, Jr., dressed in suits. Some San Franciscans were offended by the view of Rivera's ample backside facing the audience. The mural was a kind of joke, but some didn't think it was funny.

In June 1931, Kahlo and Rivera returned to Mexico, where the new president, Pascual Ortiz Rubio, wanted Rivera to continue work on the murals at the National Palace. The couple lived in the Casa Azul in Coyoacán while Rivera was building a new house for them in the San Angel section of Mexico City. It was actually two houses linked by a bridge, so that the two artists could have their privacy but still be together when they felt like it.

NEW YORK AND THE SOCIAL SCENE

Rivera went back to work on the National Palace murals, but, once again, he was interrupted, this time by an offer he couldn't refuse. The new Museum of Modern Art in New York wanted to give him a one-man show. The museum had presented only one

Rivera, Kahlo, and A. Conger Goodyear, president of New York's Museum of Modern Art, discuss Rivera's one-man show in 1931. Later, in 1938, it would be a celebrated painting of Kahlo's, not Rivera's, that would be sold at a Manhattan gallery before Goodyear could purchase it; Kahlo would paint another version just for him.

other one-man show—for Henri Matisse. He was to exhibit 143 paintings, watercolors, and drawings, as well as seven movable frescoes (wall or ceiling paintings made while the plaster is still wet).

Despite the frantic activity to prepare for the show, Kahlo and Rivera had time for a social life. They met many influential people who liked to associate with artists, including John D. and Abby Rockefeller and Lucienne and Suzanne Bloch, daughters of the Swiss composer Ernest Bloch.

Lucienne was fascinated by Rivera and at a dinner party and spent hours talking to him. "I was very impressed with Diego's idea that machines were marvelous," she said. "All the artists I knew thought machines were terrible." Once in a while, she noticed that Kahlo was giving her dark looks. Finally, Kahlo came up to her and said, "I hate you!"

"I was very impressed," Lucienne said. "This was my first contact with Frida and I loved her for it." The two women later became good friends. Lucienne went to work for Rivera as an assistant and later married another assistant. When she had her first child, Kahlo was the godmother.

Although Kahlo went along with her husband's social activities, she had strong feelings about the divisions between rich and poor that she saw in the United States. She wrote to her friend Dr. Eloesser: "High society here turns me off and I feel a bit of rage against all these rich guys here, since I have seen thousands of people in the most terrible misery without anything to eat and with no place to sleep . . . ."

Rivera's show was a big success. It attracted more visitors than any previous show at the museum. The New York critics were very favorable. One critic said Rivera was "the most talked about man on this side of the Atlantic."

Kahlo began to feel better about New York after the show closed on January 27, 1932, and her husband had more time for her. They went to parties and met many new friends. Kahlo liked to explore Manhattan and enjoyed the movies, especially the films of the Marx Brothers, Three Stooges, and Laurel and Hardy. She saw *Frankenstein* more than once.

All this was soon to come to an end, however. Rivera received commissions to paint murals in Detroit. He looked forward to being in the city where the machine was king, but Kahlo would not be happy there.

5

The Perils of "Gringolandia"

The Riveras arrived in Detroit on April 21, 1932. *The Detroit News* reported that Frida wore a black silk brocade dress with corded shirrings at the round neck, a long dark-green embroidered silk shawl, high spindle-heeled slippers, heavy dark uncut amber beads and a jadeite necklace with carved pendants. That's how newsworthy the couple had become: Kahlo's every article of clothing was news. She called herself "Carmen" in Detroit because "Frida" sounded too German, and there was a growing anti-German feeling in the country with the rise of Hitler and the Nazis. Not only did Kahlo remain in the shadow of the famous painter, she couldn't even use her own name.

Rivera had accepted a commission to paint murals celebrating the Detroit auto industry. The president of the Ford Motor Company, Edsel Ford, agreed to pay $10,000 for murals approved by the Detroit Arts Commission, which Edsel headed.

Rivera and Kahlo share a tender moment in the interior court of the Detroit Institute of Arts in 1932, where Rivera was completing a mural. Kahlo's time in Detroit was marked with difficulties; there she encountered anti-Semitism, had to hide her German ancestry, and suffered a miscarriage.

STRIKING OUT AGAINST ANTI-SEMITISM

Not long after stepping off the train in Detroit on April 21, 1932, the Riveras became involved in an old prejudice, anti-Semitism. They took up residence in the Wardell, a residential hotel across the street from the Detroit Institute of Arts. They soon discovered that the Wardell did not admit Jews. Rivera told the management that both he and Frida had Jewish blood and would have to leave.

The management was so upset that such a famous a couple would move out of their hotel that they offered to lower the rent. But Rivera demanded that the restriction against Jews be lifted or he and his wife would have to go. Not only did the management agree, they also reduced the rent from $185 to $100 a month. The Riveras had scored a victory for tolerance.

Then, at a dinner party given by automaker Henry Ford, the issue was raised again when Kahlo went up to the man whom she knew was a notorious anti-Semite and asked innocently, "Mr. Ford, are you Jewish?" Rivera thought that was uproariously funny. Ford's reaction was not recorded, but the old industrialist probably got a kick out of it, because later he and Frida tore up the dance floor together.

Kahlo's remark to Henry Ford about Jews was just one of the ways that Frida expressed her displeasure with the snobbishness of the Grosse Point people. The society women made it clear they didn't approve of Frida's manner of dress. She got back at the capitalists' wives by talking to them about the glories of Communism and, in a Catholic household, made

HENRY FORD

Henry Ford was a pioneering American industrialist. He and some partners founded the Ford Motor Company in 1903. He streamlined the manufacture of automobiles by inventing the assembly line. Ford was the first to pay his workers what was then the huge sum of $5 for an eight-hour day He also started a profit-sharing plan for his workers. He was among the first to hire and promote blacks, sometimes causing other employees to complain. He also was among the first manufacturers to hire handicapped people. He made a survey of every job in his plant to find out which could be handled by the handicapped. However, he didn't like Jews. He had anti-Semitic articles printed in his *Dearborn Independent* and promoted the nasty anti-Semitic book, *The Protocols of Zion*.

snide remarks about the Catholic Church. She even used vulgar language, pretending that she didn't know the meaning of the English words.

"What I did to those old biddies!" she would laugh later.

In a letter to Dr. Eloesser, Kahlo wrote, "This city seems to me like a shabby old village. I don't like it at all, but I am happy because Diego is working very happily here, and he has found a lot of material for his frescoes that he will do in the museum."

Frida's costumes were not always greeted with disdain. Rivera recalled how at one party all eyes were on her. Rivera always enjoyed seeing his wife the center of attention, never concerned that she was taking the limelight away from him.

While Rivera was fascinated by the factories and machines, "like a child with a new toy," Kahlo was discouraged by the shabbiness of much of Detroit, especially where the poor people lived. She noted that the poor in Mexico tended their homes with great care and had a sense of color that she didn't find in the dreary city.

PREGNANCY AND PAINTING

Frida found herself pregnant in Detroit, and she was determined to have the baby. But on the Fourth of July, 1932, she was rushed to the Henry Ford Hospital with severe bleeding. She had lost the child after two months of pregnancy. She spent 13 days in the hospital and was filled with despair. "I wish I were dead," she cried. "I don't know why I have to go on living like this."

Out of this experience, she painted one of her masterpieces, *Henry Ford Hospital*. It is grim and surrealistic, showing her bleeding on a floating bed with red ribbons linked to six suspended objects, including a fetus, two spinal columns, a snail, a strange piece of machinery, and a woman's torso. Rivera was enthusiastic about the painting, and several paintings followed it. "Frida began work on a series of masterpieces which had no precedent in the history of art—paintings which exalted the feminine qualities of endurance, of truth, reality, cruelty, and suffering," he wrote later. "Never before had a woman put such agonized poetry on canvas as Frida did in Detroit."

Another work at that time was *My Birth*, a frightening bit of surrealism in which Kahlo's mother, partially covered like a corpse, is shown giving birth to Frida, depicted as an enormous child emerging headfirst into the world. She also began experimenting with other techniques, making lithographs, painting on tin and even trying her hand at frescoes. One lithograph remains — *Frida and the Abortion*. It is a sad and potent portrait of a passive woman submitting to the various stages of pregnancy and the loss of her child. Her blood drips into the earth to fertilize a garden.

In her marriage to Rivera, Kahlo had two miscarriages and one abortion. "I lost three children," she wrote later in her life. "Paintings substituted for all this. I believe that work is the best thing." But her inability to have Rivera's child haunted her life, even though he made it clear he didn't want any more children.

At this time, Kahlo also painted *Self-Portrait on the Border Between Mexico and the United States.* She depicted the sun and the moon in the sky over the Mexican side of the painting and an American flag floating in smog on the U.S. side. The painting illustrates her feelings that the United States was a colorless place of machinery and smoke, whereas Mexico was fertile and beautiful. It also showed how anxious she was to get back home.

DEATH IN THE FAMILY

Unfortunately, when Kahlo did return it was so that she could be with her mother during her final illness. Accompanied by her friend, Lucienne Bloch, she traveled to Mexico by train and bus, a long, frustrating journey. On September 15, 1932, a week after Kahlo arrived in Coyoacán, her mother, Matilde Calderón de Kahlo, died. Frida was heartbroken, but she had to think about her father, Guillermo, who was not well either and had lapses of memory.

Kahlo stayed in Mexico for five weeks, then returned to Detroit on October 21.

While living in Detroit, Kahlo painted *Self-Portrait on the Border Between Mexico and the United States* (seen here), which expressed her ambivalence about the United States. The painting depicts contrasting symbols of Mexico—great Aztec architectural ruins and forces of nature—and the United States—mighty skyscrapers and industrial smokestacks.

BACK TO DETROIT

Kahlo didn't recognize Rivera when she got off the train in Detroit. He had dieted and lost a lot of weight. His old clothes didn't fit him anymore, and he had to borrow a suit from a friend to meet his wife. "Finally, acknowledging my identity," he wrote later, "she embraced me and began to cry."

Rivera's weight loss and the long hours he was putting in on the mural took a toll on his moods. He became irritable and rarely had time for his wife. He was racing against time because he had accepted more commissions—one for a mural in Rockefeller

Center in New York and one on the theme of *Machinery and Industry* at the 1933 World's Fair in Chicago. In addition, Rivera was active in the Mexican community of Detroit, especially in arranging transportation for Mexican workers who had come to the United States in the 1920s for work but who now, in the Great Depression, had no jobs and wanted to go home.

Meanwhile, Kahlo produced another self-portrait, this one painted on metal, a method she used from time to time. It shows a spirited and pretty Frida dressed in a white blouse with lace trim and a string of jade beads around her neck.

At this time, Kahlo was interviewed by a reporter for *The Detroit News*, who wrote that people might be surprised to discover that the wife of the famous muralist also "dabbles" in art. "No," she is quoted as saying, "I didn't study with Diego. I didn't study with anyone. I just started to paint." Although she made jokes and needled the interviewer, what she said about her origins as a painter was accurate. She never studied art formally and never apprenticed herself to anyone. Her talent was hers alone and therefore unique.

MIXED REACTIONS TO RIVERA'S MURAL

Rivera's Detroit mural caused considerable controversy. It was unveiled on March 13, 1933, and there was an immediate storm of criticism from certain circles. Church people thought it was sacrilegious; conservatives found it Communistic; others thought it was obscene. Some civic leaders threatened to wash it off the wall. The dispute was broadcast over radio and written about in newspapers. However, the general public, especially the workers who toiled making Ford automobiles and who were depicted in the painting, loved it. In fact, they took turns guarding it. And Edsel Ford, who had commissioned the work, defended Rivera. "I admire Rivera's spirit," he said. "I really believe he was trying to express his idea of the spirit of Detroit."

On a bitterly cold day in March of 1933, the Riveras and Diego's assistants arrived in Grand Central Station in New York to begin his most controversial work of all.

FIGHTING ROCKEFELLER IN NEW YORK

Kahlo was happy to be back in New York. She had many friends there, but she also appreciated the fact that New York was a port city. She had felt trapped in Detroit, but in New York she could dream about hopping on a boat to take her back to Mexico. Going home was a dream she would never lose as she made her way through the perils of "Gringolandia."

She and Rivera moved into the Barbizon-Plaza, and Rivera went to work in the RCA building. Rivera was so well known by then that people paid to watch him work. Kahlo would visit him two or three times a week, usually in the evening when the paying guests had departed. She didn't paint much during this period. She spent her time wandering around Manhattan, enjoying the department stores, the shops in Chinatown, and discount shops that were then called "dime stores."

"Frida would go through dime stores like a tornado," her friend, Lucienne Bloch, said. "Suddenly she would stop and buy something immediately. She had an extraordinary eye for the genuine and the beautiful. She'd find cheap costume jewelry and she'd make it look fantastic."

Kahlo didn't like the theater or concerts. She much preferred movies, such as Tarzan films. Once during a Tchaikovsky performance, she and Lucienne acted like rude children, making drawings and paper birds and giggling loudly.

But things started to get serious for Rivera. For some reason, it hadn't occurred to the 25-year-old Nelson Rockefeller, son of John D., Jr., future governor of New York and future vice president of the United States, that it probably wasn't a good idea to hire an avowed Communist to paint a mural in New York City, the heart of capitalism. But Rockefeller had chosen the theme for the mural himself: *Man at the Crossroads Looking with Hope and High Vision to the Choosing of a New and Better Future*. His representatives had approved of Rivera's sketches. He had liked Rivera's Detroit mural. Everything seemed fine.

But the *New York World-Telegram* took a look at the mural when it was two-thirds complete and published a story on

Nelson Rockefeller commissioned Rivera to paint the mural *Man at the Crossroads* in the newly built RCA building in New York City. The 63-foot-long mural portrays man at a symbolic crossroads of industry, science, capitalism, and Communism. Rivera included Soviet leader Vladimir Lenin as a labor leader in the painting (bottom right, wearing a suit and tie). Rockefeller unwisely commissioned the mural, not considering that Rivera's socialist views would be offensive in the city that had become the icon of American capitalism. After controversy erupted in the press over the mural in February 1934, Rockefeller had it destroyed; Rivera later recreated it in the Palace of Fine Arts in Mexico City.

April 24 with this headline: "Rivera Paints Scenes of Communist Activity and John D. Jr. Foots the Bill." The newspaper observed that the predominant color of the mural was red, the color of Communism. And it seemed to imply the victory of Communism over capitalism.

Suddenly, Rivera and his mural were in trouble. Guards started showing up. Fights broke out between the guards and Rivera's assistants. When a photographer hired by Rivera tried to take pictures of the incomplete mural, he was thrown out of the building. Eventually, Lucienne, with a camera hidden under her skirts, photographed it.

The final straw came when Rivera painted the face of Lenin on what was supposed to be the figure of a labor leader. Rockefeller, still trying to make peace with his renegade painter, urged him to substitute the face of an unknown man for Lenin. Rivera, of course, refused. However, he did offer to balance Lenin by painting the face of Abraham Lincoln on another figure. Rockefeller didn't bother to reply. Instead, his rental manager, accompanied by 12 uniformed security guards, arrived at the building on May 9 and ordered Rivera to stop working. When the artist climbed down from his scaffolding, he was handed a check for $14,000, the remainder of what Rockefeller owed him on the $21,000 contract. The scaffolding was taken down and workers covered the mural with tar paper and a wooden screen.

The controversy raged. Mounted police had to be called when Rivera's supporters arrived to picket Rockefeller Center. Pickets also went to Rockefeller's home. They carried signs that read, "Save Rivera's Painting," and "We want Rockefeller with a rope around his neck! Freedom in art!" A group of artists and intellectuals, including some of the leading figures in art and literature of the time, petitioned Rockefeller to save the mural. Of course, Rockefeller had the final say.

Rivera got more bad news a few days later when his friend, architect Albert Kahn, who designed the General Motors Building at the Chicago World's Fair, sent him a telegram saying his commission to paint the *Forge and Foundry* mural at the fair had been cancelled.

Kahlo had done everything she could think of to save the RCA mural. She wrote letters and attended protest meetings. A few months later, she ran into Nelson Rockefeller at the opening of Sergei Eisenstein's film, *Que Viva Mexico!* Rockefeller was cordial. "How are you, Frida?" he asked. She turned on her heel and marched off. However, Frida's enemies were usually only temporary. Seven years later in 1940, she ran into Rockefeller in Mexico when he was making arrangements for an exhibition, "Twenty Centuries of Mexican Art," at the Museum of Modern Art in New York. A photograph shows her sitting next to him at a luncheon.

COMMUNISM IN AMERICA

It's important to know that Communism had a strong appeal to some Americans who were suffering in the Great Depression. It seemed to them that the capitalist system of private ownership was not working and maybe it was time to try something else. Socialists wanted government ownership of the means of production, and Communists wanted the workers to be in charge. They believed that the government eventually would "wither away" under Communism and workers' groups would take over and everybody would live in peace and freedom. Many of those who got involved in Communism regretted it later when they discovered that the Soviet Union did not really have a Communist government under Josef Stalin and that it was just another ruthless dictatorship. Among those who fought against Stalin was Leon Trotsky, who would soon play an important role in the lives of Diego Rivera and Frida Kahlo.

HOMESICK IN NEW YORK

After the turmoil over the Rockefeller Center mural, Kahlo was anxious to go back to Mexico. She and Rivera fought long and loudly over the issue. He wanted to stay in New York, where he was a popular figure and hailed wherever he went. But there was no glory for Kahlo in Manhattan. She had not been very creative there. Toward the end of their nine months in New York, she managed to start a painting, *My Dress Hangs There*, which she finished in Mexico. It is a sad piece of work, showing her empty Tehuana dress hanging on a ribbon stretched between two columns. On one of the columns is a toilet; on the other, a sports trophy. All around are images of the big city, including a poster of Mae West, churches (with the cross turned into a dollar sign), apartment and office buildings, including one on fire, and a trash can brimming with discarded junk and human parts and topped by a bloody hand. Looming over all is Federal Hall on Wall Street with the statue of George Washington out front. At the top is the port, showing the Statue of Liberty and a ship steaming away. No doubt, Kahlo pictured her homesick self on that boat.

Rivera had many friends in New York, including more than a few women. They followed him around like little puppies, and there's no doubt he became intimately involved with some. Kahlo not only yearned for Mexico, she wasn't feeling well. Her foot was partially paralyzed and she hated the summer heat. She spent most of the day in the bathtub. Then November came, and the first snow fell. She was not looking forward to winter in New York. She yearned for her sunny homeland.

"New York is very pretty and I feel better here than in Detroit," she wrote to a friend, "but in spite of this, I am longing for Mexico."

Rivera, who always had a violent temper, once picked up a painting he had done of a Mexican desert landscape and shouted, "I don't want to go back to that!" He took a knife and cut it into shreds before the horrified eyes of Kahlo and some friends.

Nevertheless, on December 20, 1933, Kahlo finally got on board a ship like the one in her painting. She and Rivera returned to Mexico on the *Oriente*. Her return to Mexico was not to be the happy time that she had looked forward to.

6

"A Few Little Pricks"

Kahlo was glad to be back in Mexico, but Rivera was not at all happy about it. He hadn't wanted to give up the attention and acclaim he was getting from the New York artists and intellectuals. He sulked for months, refused to work and made Kahlo's life miserable by blaming her for dragging him back to Mexico against his will.

They moved into the double house in the San Angel section of Mexico City. It consisted of one big house for Rivera, including a high-ceilinged studio where he could not only work but entertain guests and exhibit his work for sale. Kahlo's house was smaller but also had a studio on the third floor with a big picture window. Rivera's house was painted pink; Kahlo's blue. A bridge linked the two houses.

RIVERA'S INFIDELITY

Neither artist did much work in 1934, and then Kahlo was devastated to learn that Rivera was having an affair with her younger sister, Cristina. Rivera had used Cristina as a model for nudes in some of

Kahlo welcomes Leon Trotsky (second from right) and his wife, Natalia, with the leader of the American Communist Committee, Max Shachtman, to Mexico. Trotsky and his wife accepted the refuge Rivera arranged for them in the country, and stayed at Kahlo's Coyoacán home. Kahlo, characteristically attracted to this powerful socialist leader, soon became entangled in an extramarital affair with Trotsky.

his murals and the relationship apparently developed from there. Possibly in reaction, Kahlo's first painting after that dry period was of a woman who had been stabbed to death by her boyfriend. It was entitled *A Few Little Pricks* because when the killer went before the judge he said, "But I only gave her a few little pricks." The gruesome painting shows the naked woman on a bed bleeding from numerous stab wounds while the killer stands over her. Some thought Kahlo saw herself in the brutalized woman. She, too, was suffering from the "little pricks" that Rivera had been delivering for years by his bad behavior.

Rivera freely admitted that he treated women horribly. In his autobiography, he wrote: "If I loved a woman, the more I loved her, the more I wanted to hurt her. Frida was only the most obvious victim of this disgusting trait."

Both Kahlo and Rivera suffered physical problems the first year they were back in Mexico. Rivera was still suffering the effects of the severe diet he went on in New York. In fact, a doctor ordered the man who once weighed 300 pounds to gain some weight. Kahlo had an appendectomy (surgery to remove her appendix) and had another miscarriage, this one after three months of pregnancy. Her right foot kept giving her trouble, and she finally agreed to have all five toes amputated.

Rivera finally got back to work on the frescoes at the National Palace. But he added insult to injury by painting Cristina and Frida in one scene, making Cristina far more attractive and important figure than Frida.

Frida wrote to Dr. Eloesser, "I'm so down and discouraged now, so unhappy that I don't know how I'm going to go on. I realize that Diego is now more interested in her (Cristina) than me and I keep saying to myself that I have to be ready to accept compromises if I want him to be happy. But it's costing me so much to put up with all this and you can't imagine how I'm suffering." Even in her suffering, however, Kahlo's main concern still seemed to be how to make Rivera happy.

Kahlo continued for several years to depict in paintings her suffering over Rivera's affair with her sister. In *Memory* (1937), she shows herself standing next to an enormous bleeding heart on the ground. Dangling from ribbons are her colorful Tehuana costume on her left and her schoolgirl dress on her right. She herself is seen with short-cropped hair wearing a white skirt and blouse and jacket. In one hand, she is holding a liquor bottle, indicating that she was drinking heavily at the time. Frida did cut off her long, dark hair after discovering Rivera's relationship with her sister. But she let it grow back later.

Finally, Kahlo could not stand living with Rivera any longer and moved to an apartment on Avenida Insurgentes in the center of Mexico City. There, her old boyfriend, Alejandro Gómez Arias, visited her. He related later how Frida looked out the window and saw her sister, Cristina, getting gas in her car across the street.

"Look!" Arias quoted her as saying. "Come here! Why does she come and fill up her car in front of my house?"

Kahlo would eventually forgive her sister, but the hurt of Rivera's betrayal continued for many years. Kahlo herself had romantic relationships with both men and women during this period. One intense affair was with the American sculptor Isamu Noguchi, who had come to Mexico to paint a mural. Noguchi said of Frida, "I loved her very much. She was a lovely person, absolutely marvelous person. Since Diego was well known to be a lady chaser, she cannot be blamed if she saw some men. In those days we all sort of, more or less, horsed around, and Diego did and so did Frida."

As if to prove that she had not lost her spirit, Kahlo and two women friends decided on an impulse to fly to New York. The flight was a disaster. The plane was forced to land several times, and they finished the trip by train. But she enjoyed being back in Manhattan, even if only for a short visit. It was there, according to her friend, Bertram Wolfe, that Frida realized that, despite everything, it was Rivera she truly loved.

"As the flames of resentment died down," Wolfe wrote later, "she knew it was Diego she loved and that he meant more to her than the things that seemed to stand between them."

But Kahlo's romance with Leon Trotsky was the strangest of her relationships.

TROTSKY SEEKS ASYLUM

Trotsky was one of the leaders of the Russian Revolution in 1917. He and Vladimir Lenin were Bolsheviks, members of the revolutionary party that took over the country when Czar Nicholas II abdicated (left office). The Russian czar ruled the country like a king or emperor. Nicholas and his whole family were later killed by revolutionaries.

Trotsky had spent time in prison, including Siberia, for earlier revolutionary activities. But he had escaped and lived in other countries at different times, including the United States. When Lenin returned to Russia from Germany, where he had been living, Trotsky joined him. Trotsky became Lenin's right-hand man. But after Lenin became ill in 1922, Josef Stalin took power. Stalin and Trotsky turned into bitter enemies, and Stalin ordered him out of the country in 1929.

Trotsky had become friends with Diego Rivera, who put him and Lenin in two murals, the *Communist Unity Panel* at the New Workers School in New York, and *Man, Controller of the Universe* in Mexico City. So, when Trotsky had trouble finding a country that would take him in, Rivera intervened on his behalf with the Mexican government.

Rivera was a Trotskyite. He had met Stalin during a visit to the Soviet Union in 1927 and didn't like him. Rivera's fellow muralist, David Alfaro Siqueiros, was a Stalinist. The two got into violent arguments over the subject.

By this time, Lazaro Cardenas had been elected president of Mexico and sent the country back to its original revolutionary ideals—land and labor reforms. He kicked president Plutarco Elías Calles out of the country in 1936 because he was against such reforms.

Rivera used his influence with the new government to give Trotsky political asylum (safety) in Mexico. On November 9, 1937, Trotsky and his wife, Natalia, arrived in the harbor of Tampico aboard the oil tanker *Ruth*. Frida Kahlo, representing her husband, was among a party of dignitaries who met the couple. Rivera was in the hospital suffering from eye and kidney problems.

Trotsky was heavily guarded. He and his wife were aware that Stalin wanted him dead. In fact, Natalia was so terrified of possible killers that she refused to get off the ship until she saw some familiar faces. Trotsky was 57, tall and energetic. He made friends wherever he went, and he easily charmed his hosts. They went to live in Kahlo's home in Coyoacán, where her father still lived. Guillermo Kahlo was a little puzzled by this event. He had never heard of Trotsky. He said to his daughter, "You esteem this person, don't you? I want to talk to him. I want to advise him not to get involved with politics. Politics are very bad." Later, Guillermo Kahlo moved in with his daughter and Frida's sister, Adriana.

But Trotsky wouldn't have taken Guillermo's advice. He was busy working on a biography of Lenin and forming an international commission to analyze the evidence used by Stalin to evict him from the Communist Party and the Soviet Union. The commission, headed by the American educator John Dewey, actually held a kind of trial in the Coyoacán house. It was attended by representatives of many countries and was covered by the press. At the end of the sessions, the commission declared Trotsky innocent of the charges against him.

While the trial was in session, guards stood outside the house, and windows facing the street were covered with adobe bricks. To make the house even more secure, Rivera bought the

LEON TROTSKY

Leon Trotsky was in New York when he heard that Russian Czar Nicholas II had been overthrown by revolutionaries. It was 1917, and he hurried back to Moscow to help Vladimir Lenin form a Bolshevik government. The Communist Party in Russia had its origins in 1898, when the Russian Socialist Democratic Labor Party held secret meetings. The party's ideas were based on the teachings of Karl Marx. Lenin's faction was known as the *Bolsheviki* (members of the majority). Another faction was the *Mensheviki* (the minority). The Bolsheviks prevailed and became the Russian Communist Party in 1918. Trotsky and Lenin were the leaders. But when Lenin became ill, Josef Stalin took over the party and Trotsky was ousted.

property next door, evicted the family that lived there, and connected the two dwellings. Rivera was now a member of the International Communist League, a Trotskyite organization.

AFFIR WITH TROTSKY

Trotsky was very much interested in women. He tried to get close to Cristina, but she wanted no part of him. Kahlo, however, found the revolutionary hero very attractive, and he soon returned the affection. She was then 29 and, from photographs and her own self-portrait, quite beautiful. She and Trotsky began meeting in Cristina's home on Aguayo Street. Although Rivera seemed ignorant of the affair, Natalia Trotsky soon found out about it.

Trotsky moved to a farm near San Miguel Regla, about 80 miles northeast of Mexico City. After a visit there with other friends, Kahlo broke off the relationship. Trotsky was upset and wrote her a nine-page letter telling her how much she meant to him. But it was all over.

On November 7, 1937, the anniversary of the Russian Revolution and Trotsky's birthday, Kahlo gave Trotsky a self-portrait, showing her standing between two curtains holding in one hand a bouquet of flowers and in the other a note that says: "For Leon Trotsky with all love I dedicate this painting on the 7th of November, 1937. Frida Kahlo in San Angel, Mexico."

André Breton, the French surrealist poet, described Kahlo in the portrait after he saw it in Trotsky's study: "She has painted herself dressed in a robe of wings gilded with butterflies . . . We are privileged to be present . . . at the entry of a young woman endowed with all the gifts of seduction, one accustomed to the society of men of genius."

After the romance with Trotsky was over, Kahlo became more productive than she had been in years. She produced more paintings in 1937 and 1938 than she had during the entire eight years of her marriage. Exhibits and sales awaited her, as well as visits to New York and Paris. Other tragic things were ahead of her, however.

KAHLO'S PAINTINGS SELL

Edward G. Robinson was the tough-guy actor of the American screen from the 1930s into the 1970s. One of his most famous roles was as the gangster in *Little Caesar* in 1930. But not many of his fans knew that he was an art collector with excellent taste. He was one of the first to buy Frida Kahlo's paintings.

It was Rivera who arranged for Robinson to see Kahlo's art when the actor and his wife, Gladys, were visiting Mexico. "I kept about 28 paintings hidden," Kahlo wrote later. "While I was on the roof terrace with Mrs. Robinson, Diego showed him my paintings and Robinson bought four of them from me for $200 each." She suddenly realized that she could make money selling her art. "For me it was such a surprise that I marveled and said: 'This way I am going to be able to be free, I'll be able to travel and do what I want without asking Diego for money.'"

Some of Kahlo's paintings were included in a group show in 1938 at the University Gallery in Mexico City. Someone who saw them there told Manhattan gallery owner Julien Levy about them. He wrote to Kahlo and said he was interested in showing her work at his gallery. She sent him some photographs of her paintings, and he wrote back saying he wanted to show 30 of her works that October. Ever modest about her paintings, Kahlo later told a friend, "I don't know what they see in my work. Why do they want me to have a show?" But she accepted the invitation.

Kahlo and Rivera drew up a list of important people to invite to the exhibit. It included some of the more important and famous people in the arts, business, and educational circles. Among them were Nelson Rockefeller and his father John D. Rockefeller, Jr. Obviously, the Riveras didn't hold grudges, at least when it came to possible purchasers of Frida's art.

Kahlo went alone to New York. André Breton, who insisted that Kahlo was a fellow surrealist, had written a glowing introduction to the show for the catalogue. The fact that it was printed in the original French annoyed some people. At any rate, Kahlo did not consider herself a surrealist, a movement in both art and literature in which reality is distorted into dream-like shapes and images. In fact, Kahlo did not like to link herself with any school of art. She considered her paintings to be uniquely her own.

"They thought I was a surrealist," she once said, "but I wasn't. I never painted dreams. I painted my own reality."

But while the New York show was proceeding, the surrealist, Breton, was arranging an exhibit for her in Paris.

A reviewer for *Time* magazine wrote of the New York exhibit: "Little Frida's pictures, mostly painted in oil on copper, had the daintiness of miniatures, the vivid reds and yellows of Mexican tradition and the playfully bloody fancy of an unsentimental child."

About half of Kahlo's paintings sold. A. Conger Goodyear, president of the Museum of Modern Art, fell in love with Kahlo's painting of herself with her monkey, Fulang-Chang. But it had been sold to someone else. So Kahlo sat in her hotel room at the Barbizon-Plaza and produced another picture of herself with her monkey just for Goodyear. Kahlo loved animals and had many pets, including several monkeys and parrots. She often painted herself with these creatures.

An example of Kahlo's independence as an artist came when the playwright Claire Booth Luce, wife of Henry Luce, who was the founder of *Time* magazine, asked her to paint a remembrance of Luce's friend, Dorothy Hale, who had committed suicide. Luce wanted a nice, warm painting that she could give to Hale's mother. But what Kahlo produced was so shocking, Luce couldn't even look at it. It showed Hale plunging from a tall building and lying bloody on the ground. It might have been a masterpiece, but it certainly wasn't what Luce had in mind. She had it locked away for decades, and no one saw it until a friend of Luce's donated it to the Phoenix Art Museum.

Despite all of her relationships with other men, Kahlo still loved Diego Rivera above all and worried about him constantly. In fact, she was reluctant to go to Paris for the exhibit André Breton had organized because she didn't want to leave Rivera in Mexico alone.

Kahlo's self-portrait with her monkey, Fulang-Chang, was one of 30 paintings shown at her first gallery exhibition in October 1938. A. Conger Goodyear, the president of the Museum of Modern Art who showed Rivera's paintings seven years earlier, loved the painting so much that, when it was sold to someone else before he could purchase it, Kahlo produced another one specifically for him.

KAHLO TAKES PARIS

Rivera wrote to her in New York: "I don't want you for my sake to lose the opportunity to go to Paris. Take from life all which she gives you, whatever it may be, provided it is interesting and can give you some pleasure."

Kahlo arrived in Paris in January 1939. The start of World

War II was only months away, and the world was on edge. In addition, the Paris exhibition started out as a disaster. For one thing Breton, whom Kahlo didn't really like very much, was making a botch of organizing the show. Finally, the artist Marcel Duchamp, whom Kahlo said was the only one "who has his feet on the earth," took over. He found a gallery for the show, which was called *Mexique*. But Kahlo was taken ill and had to be hospitalized with a kidney infection. She wrote to Nickolas Murray that she was about to get out of Paris "before I get nuts myself."

She stayed, however, and the show opened March 10 at the Pierre Colle gallery. Her paintings were well received by the critics. And the Louvre, the foremost French museum of art, purchased one of her self-portraits, *The Frame*. Rivera wrote later that the Russian artist Wassily Kandinsky "was so moved by Frida's paintings that, right before everyone in the exhibition room, he lifted her in his arms and kissed her cheeks and brow while tears of sheer emotion ran down his face." Although Rivera was not there, he got the information about the show second-hand. He also wrote that Picasso "sang the praises of Frida's artistic and personal qualities. From the moment he met her until she left for home, Picasso was under her spell."

That was probably true. Picasso gave Kahlo a pair of tiny tortoise-shell earrings in the shape of hands with gold cuffs and taught her a Spanish song. She used the earrings in paintings and enjoyed singing the song for friends.

Kahlo became something of a celebrity within Parisian artistic circles and attracted wide attention with her Tehuana costumes. In fact, Elsa Schiaparelli, the well-known Italian designer, created a *robe Madame Rivera* for fashionable Parisians. And Kahlo's hands, with her flashy jade and silver rings on her fingers, appeared on the cover of *Vogue*.

Meanwhile, Rivera and Trotsky had had a falling out in Mexico. They disagreed heatedly over political matters, and Rivera resigned from the Trotskyite Fourth International. Trotsky even wrote to Kahlo, seeking her help in healing their differences. She did not respond.

Strangely, Kahlo met the man who would kill Trotsky. While in Paris, she ran into Ramon Mercader, who was also known as Jacques Mornard. He made a pass at her, which she rebuffed. She related later that Mercader, who pretended to be a Trotskyite, asked her to find him a house near Trotsky in Mexico. She told him to find his own house. Mercader was actually an agent of the Soviet secret service, GPU, and he had been assigned by Stalin to kill Trotsky, which he did on August 20, 1940.

Kahlo's stay in Paris had its ups and downs, but she basically enjoyed the attention she received from some of the leading lights of the Parisian art world. Actually, the lights of France were soon to go out. World War II began on September 1, 1939, when Germany invaded Poland. They were not to go back on until the liberation of Paris in 1945. But Kahlo escaped all that by returning to Mexico. She left Le Havre, France, for Mexico on March 25 by ship. Not long after her arrival, Rivera told her he wanted a divorce.

DIVORCE

No one was sure why Diego Rivera suddenly wanted to divorce his wife. There was speculation that he had found out about her affair with Trotsky. There was also speculation that she had found out about his possible affair with the American movie actress Paulette Goddard, who lived for a time in a hotel across from his San Angel studio. There is a photograph showing him and the Hungarian painter Irene Bohus painting portraits of Goddard. There was also a rumor that Rivera planned to marry Bohus.

As often happened to Kahlo, she and her husband's mistress, Paulette Goddard, became friends. She painted a still life, *The Flower Basket*, for Goddard in 1941.

Whatever the cause of the divorce, the couple began the proceedings on September 19, 1939. Kahlo's old school friend, Manuel Gonzalez Ramirez, was her lawyer, and the divorce was made final the next month. Rivera told the press that the divorce was only a matter of "legal convenience." He told *Time* magazine that it was done "in order to improve Frida's legal position . . . purely a matter of legal convenience in the spirit of modern

Kahlo's self-portrait, *The Two Fridas*, completed shortly after her divorce from Rivera, expresses her anguish over her marital crisis. The Mexican Frida, who was loved by Rivera, wears a colorful Tehuana dress; one end of her artery is connected to a miniature portrait of Rivera in her hand, signifying that his love has kept her alive. Her other artery connects the Mexican Frida to her more European counterpart; this Frida wears a white lace dress, and having been rejected by her lover, holds no mementos of him. A surgical clamp on her exposed artery is the only thing preventing her from bleeding to death—this Kahlo will not survive long without her beloved.

times." He added that there was "no change in the magnificent relations between us."

Kahlo herself told a reporter that there were "intimate reasons, personal causes, difficult to explain," for the divorce.

Rivera continued to honor his ex-wife when talking to reporters. He said he considered her "among the five or six most prominent modernist painters."

Meanwhile, Kahlo's art career was blooming. On the day that the divorce papers came through, she had nearly finished one of her most famous paintings, *The Two Fridas*. The two figures of herself sit side by side. One is dressed as a European lady; the other in her famous Tehuana costume. They are holding hands. In both figures, the hearts are exposed and linked by a blood-filled artery. The European figure holds a clamp and is trying to stop the flow of blood that threatens to destroy them both. Drops of blood drip on her white skirt. The Tehuana Frida also holds a miniature painting of Diego Rivera as a child. *The Two Fridas* was one of her biggest works, at 67 by 67 inches.

That painting and *The Wounded Table* were exhibited at the International Surrealism Exhibition organized by the Gallery of Mexican Art in Mexico City in January 1940. In *The Wounded Table*, Kahlo is seated at a long table on what looks like a theater stage, accompanied by her niece and nephew, Isolda and Antonio Kahlo, her pet fawn, El Granizo (hail), a Judas figure (a figure symbolizing evil forces), a pre-Columbian (produced before the arrival of Christopher Columbus in the New World in 1492) idol, and a skeleton. Blood is dripping everywhere, and the painting is seen as a message to Rivera, showing how he has wounded her. The Judas figures were a Mexican tradition. They were made of papier-mâché and were meant to be burned as effigies (representations of despised figures) during the season of Lent.

The Two Fridas was exhibited later in New York in the Museum of Modern Art's exhibition, *Twenty Centuries of Mexican Art*. It was sold to the Institute of Fine Arts in Mexico, but not until seven years later. *The Wounded Table* had a more interesting history. It was exhibited in Warsaw, Poland, in 1955, then reportedly sent to the Soviet Union as a gift from the Mexican Communist Party. What happened to it after that is not known.

Artist of
the Casa Azul

Someone once asked Kahlo why she painted so many self-portraits. She replied, "Because I am alone."

Many of Kahlo's paintings depict her as wounded. Some reflect the streetcar accident that left her damaged; others seem to refer to the wounds inflicted on her by men and life in general. One is *Self-Portrait With Thorny Necklace,* in which the thorns cut into her neck as her monkey and cat look on. A dead hummingbird dangles from the necklace. Another, even more gruesome painting is *The Broken Column.* It is another self-portrait, this one showing her with nails driven into her face and body. Kahlo's exposed spine is bound together with straps. Tears pour from her eyes.

Besides such gory works, Kahlo was capable of producing beautiful portraits, including a sensitive one of Doña Rosita Morillo Safa, an elderly woman shown knitting with flowering cacti behind her. Kahlo was commissioned to paint that portrait by Safa's son,

76

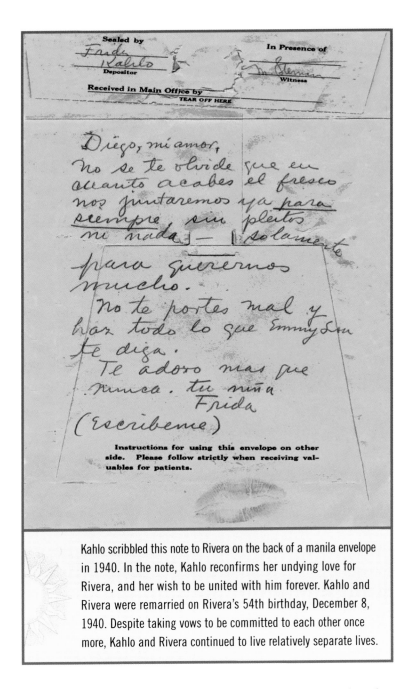

Kahlo scribbled this note to Rivera on the back of a manila envelope in 1940. In the note, Kahlo reconfirms her undying love for Rivera, and her wish to be united with him forever. Kahlo and Rivera were remarried on Rivera's 54th birthday, December 8, 1940. Despite taking vows to be committed to each other once more, Kahlo and Rivera continued to live relatively separate lives.

Eduardo Morillo Safa, an engineer and diplomat, who also paid her to paint portraits of other members of his family, all beautifully done.

Many of Kahlo's still-lifes, such as the painting of flowers that she did for Paulette Goddard and one called *Life, How I Love You*, of plump melons and other fruit, capture her unique sense of beauty and reverence for life.

Then there is the remarkable *What the Water Gave Me*, which is a view of a tub of water as seen from someone, presumably Kahlo, lying in it. Her feet are pressed against the far end of the tub. In between, floating in the water, are images of her parents at their wedding ceremony, a building erupting from a volcano, her empty Tehuana dress, and scenes of love and abandonment.

Many of Frida's self-portraits over the years show her with closely cropped hair. That's because every time she got angry at Rivera, who loved her long black tresses, she chopped them off.

Frida's health deteriorated after her divorce. In addition to being upset by the murder of Trotsky and the fact that police questioned her about it because she had known the killer, she was drinking heavily and was in constant pain from her old injuries and sicknesses. In September 1940, she flew to San Francisco for treatment by her old friend Dr. Eloesser. He prescribed rest, a special diet, and other therapies and told her to stop drinking. Her health improved greatly after that visit.

While in San Francisco, she showed her work at the Golden Gate International Exhibition.

REMARRIAGE TO RIVERA

Eloesser also urged Rivera and Kahlo to get back together. On Rivera's 54th birthday, December 8, 1940, they were married again. Kahlo was 33.

Despite being married again, Kahlo was determined to live an independent life. She moved back to the Casa Azul in Coyoacán, while Rivera remained in the double house in San Angel.

Kahlo hung a skeleton next to her bed and gave it a handshake and affectionate greeting every morning. She also kept a fetus in formaldehyde in a jar on her bookshelf. She told visitors it was her own stillborn child. She might have been kidding. She had an eccentric sense of humor. She also had a large collection of pre-Columbian figures, art objects, curios, dolls, and toys. Kahlo always asked friends who were going to take trips to bring her back a toy. Huge Judas figures were placed in various rooms and on the patio. There is a photo of her and Rivera standing with one of these figures, which appears to be about 12 feet tall.

Rivera added a wing to the Casa Azul. It was made of volcanic rock and decorated with stone mosaics. The largest room was Kahlo's studio. Her many pets, including monkeys, birds, her deer, a dog, and other creatures could run freely through the house. Her bedroom was a remarkable place. The bed, in which she spent a great deal of time because of her illnesses, had an overhead mirror. The headboard was completely covered with photographs of family and friends. There were portraits of Karl Marx and Friedrich Engels, whose ideas led to the development of Communism, as well as Lenin, Stalin, and Mao Tse-tung (pronounced zee-dong), the Communist leader of China. She still used the wooden easel her mother had rigged up for her years ago to paint while lying in bed.

Frida's father, Guillermo Kahlo, died in 1941. His death was one more blow in a life that had seen many setbacks and disappointments. Nevertheless, during the 1940s, she painted a series of remarkable self-portraits. *Self-Portrait as a Tehuana (Diego in My Thoughts)* shows her in an elaborate Tehuana headdress with a picture of Rivera on her forehead. A similar painting, entitled simply *Self-Portrait,* shows her in a similar finely wrought headpiece with tears dripping from her eyes.

The hummingbird shows up again in a 1946 self-portrait, its outstretched wings form her dramatic eyebrows. Another from 1943 has her posed against a riot of vines and leaves with a picture of a skull and bone on her forehead. It is entitled *Thinking of Death.* A portrait from 1949 shows a much darker image

In *Self-Portrait with Diego on My Breast* (1953/54) Kahlo invokes a
device she frequently used to communicate her emotions explicitly:
by placing small portraits of Rivera on her body to signify his
effect on her. Kahlo also used this technique in the 1940s, as in
Self-Portrait as a Tehuana (Diego in My Thoughts) where Rivera
is placed symbolically on her forehead. In the above *Self-Portrait
with Rivera on My Breast*, Kahlo's love for Rivera is conveyed by
his placement over her heart.

of Kahlo with a larger picture of Rivera on her forehead. This time he has a third eye in the middle of his own forehead. (A third eye signifies wisdom.) Her rich black hair swirls about her neck. And once again tears are dripping from her eyes. It is entitled *Diego and I.* She also painted numerous other self-portraits with her various pets, mostly monkeys and parrots.

Claire Booth Luce was not the only one who was unhappy upon receiving a commissioned painting from Kahlo. Mexican President Avila Camacho paid her to do *Still Life,* but turned it down when he saw it. It is an image of a grotesquely overripe melon, its innards exposed, surrounded by other fruit and a large butterfly. Kahlo often used overripe or broken fruit to represent her own body that had been cut and torn over the years by accidents and surgery.

Still, Kahlo was becoming famous. In 1942, her paintings were included in an exhibition at New York's Museum of Modern Art entitled *Twentieth-Century Portraits.* Her work also was included in a New York exhibition of 31 women artists at Peggy Guggenheim's Art of This Century Gallery in January 1943, and in an exhibit of Mexican art at the Philadelphia Museum of Art that same year. Her portrait of Marucha Lavin, a circular work 25 inches in diameter, was included in a group show at the Benjamin Franklin Library in Mexico City entitled *A Century of the Portrait in Mexico, 1830-1942.*

In 1943, Kahlo and Rivera taught art at the Education Ministry's School of Painting and Sculpture, known as La Esmeralda. On her first day at the school, Kahlo asked the students what they wanted to paint. They asked her to pose for them. One student, Guillermo Monroy, gave possibly the best description of what Kahlo was like at that time:

> Frida was there in front of us, amazingly still. Her hands, placed one of top of the other, were elegant and bedecked with rings. Her beautifully manicured fingernails were long and lacquered with bright red polish. Her silky black hair was criss-crossed on top of her head in meticulous braids,

beautifully decorated in the center with a tiny bunch of gaudy magenta bougainvillea. Her filigree earrings were two small suns made of gold. Smooth skin, firm and cool. Dark, restless eyes seeing beyond earth and sky, black eyebrows joining to form the delicate wings of a bird. The freshest of smiles flowering on her red lips. Was it any wonder that many men were attracted to her over the years?

Kahlo wanted her students to go their own way in art. She rarely looked over their shoulders. She encouraged them to go out in the street to find subjects to paint.

"We all went to the markets, the factories, the country-side, we mixed with the people," Monroy said. "Frida told us that direct contact with life and participation in it, not as mere spectators, but as socially active citizens, would open new artistic horizons and greatly enrich our aesthetic and human sensitivity."

Kahlo was a popular teacher, and many of her students continued to study with her at the Casa Azul in Coyoacán when she was unable to make it to school. Four of her most devoted students were known as *Los Fridos,* in honor of their teacher.

Meanwhile, Rivera was back to work at the National Palace, this time painting panels of early Mexican civilizations. He frequently included Kahlo in his murals. He also worked on a mural at the Institute of Cardiology, a two-wall fresco on the theme of religion versus science.

Kahlo's health gradually deteriorated through the 1940s, but in many ways the five years after her remarriage were possibly the happiest and most productive of her life. In 1946, she went to New York for surgery on her spine, which was probably botched and only added to her pain.

FINAL PAINTINGS

In 1942, as most of the rest of the world was torn by war, Rivera launched a project to build a sort of temple-museum to house his collection of treasures of Mexico's ancient history. It was also

Kahlo sits on the patio of the Casa Azul in Coyoacán, where her students would come to study when she was in too much pain to travel to the Education Ministry's School of Painting and Sculpture, known as La Esmeralda. A popular teacher, Kahlo encouraged her students to become socially active citizens through which she believed they could draw their artistic inspiration. Her four most devoted students called themselves *Los Fridos* in honor of their beloved mentor.

meant to be a ranch where he and Kahlo could be independent of a world they both saw as gradually going mad. They would live there, raise animals and their own fruits and vegetables, and be self-sufficient.

It was called Anahuacalli, and it turned out to be a strange, gloomy stone mausoleum-like structure set on a lava bed in the Pedregal (stony ground) district near Coyoacán. Kahlo and Rivera never lived there and probably never planted anything there either, but Kahlo became as passionate about Anahuacalli as her husband. She contributed her own money to help build it and tried without success to get the Mexican government to chip in. It was finally opened to the public as a museum in 1964, long after both were dead.

As Kahlo's health continued to worsen in the 1940s, her fame spread. The Casa Azul was visited by people from all walks of life—show business, the arts, politics, and business. Even the Rockefellers came by, as did the famous dancer Josephine Baker and the Mexican film star Dolores del Rio. The visitors always got a delicious meal and were treated to Frida's unquenchable good humor. Even later, when confined to a wheelchair, she made people feel good by just being in their presence. Kahlo's family was an exception. Her mother's sisters refused to visit her and would not let their children go to the house. After all, as far as they were concerned, the Riveras were living in sin. They were not married in the church, *and* they were Communists. Her aunts actually sprinkled holy water on the sidewalk outside the "house of sin." But the two children of Frida's sister Cristina, Isolda and Antonio, were good company and also appeared in at least one of Aunt Frida's paintings. Every year, Frida held *posadas,* the traditional

NELSON ROCKEFELLER

Nelson Rockefeller was the grandson of John D. Rockefeller, who founded the Standard Oil Company. He was director of Rockefeller Center from 1931 to 1958. He held a number of federal government jobs, including coordinator of the Office of Inter-American Affairs, chairman of the International Development Advisory Board, and chairman of the President's Advisory Committee on Government Organization. He defeated Averell Harriman for governorship of New York in 1958 and was reelected three times. In 1974, he became vice president of the United States under President Gerald Ford, who had been Richard M. Nixon's vice president when Nixon resigned. He died in 1979.

Christmas season parties, with piñatas for the children to break, fireworks, and colorful decorations and food. In 1946, Kahlo received the National Prize of Arts and Sciences from the Education Ministry. It carried a 5,000 peso prize. It was awarded for her painting, *Moses*. She painted it after reading Freud's *Moses and Monotheism*. It is an unusual work for her, somewhat resembling Rivera's mural art. It is crowded with images—a snail, a skeleton, and images of great figures from history, including Jesus, Karl Marx, Gandhi, Napoleon, and Stalin, as well as nudes, Greek, Egyptian, and Aztec gods and goddesses, a fetus, and gnarled trees—all surrounding the infant Moses floating in a basket on the Nile under what looks like a boiling sun. Rivera usually crowded his murals with images, mostly of people in action, but it was unusual for Kahlo to jam so much into her paintings. *Moses* also is one of her largest paintings—30 by 24 inches.

Kahlo also followed the style of the *exvotos*, religious paintings on metal usually by unknown artists, which were donated to churches as offerings. Often the art would include text, describing what was going on in the painting. Kahlo frequently included text in her artworks in the same manner.

In June 1946, Frida and Cristina flew to New York where Frida underwent a bone graft operation at the Hospital for Special Surgery. Four of her vertebrae were fused, and a metal rod was inserted to strengthen her spine. There was some evidence that the doctors fused the wrong vertebrae. She was in severe pain and required massive doses of morphine. Taking drugs, as well as drinking large amounts of alcohol, became a daily procedure in her final years. But Kahlo continued painting. She finished *Tree of Hope, Stay Strong* that year. It shows her in her Tehuana costume standing guard over another Frida, lying on a gurney (stretcher) with deep wounds in her back. The same year, she painted *The Little Deer*, a picture of a deer with Frida's head, pierced and bleeding from many arrows. The next year, Kahlo painted *Self-Portrait with Loose Hair*, in which the famous, saucy Frida now looks tired and drawn.

One of Kahlo's most amazing paintings at this time was *The Love Embrace of the Universe, the Earth (Mexico), Diego, Me and Senor Xolotl* (a pet deer). It shows her holding a naked Diego Rivera (with a large third eye), curled up like a child, in the embrace of huge arms, one dark and one light. Many of her later paintings depicted a dark and light world, signifying life and death.

Strangely, Kahlo painted a portrait of her father in 1951, 10 years after his death, with his camera beside him. She painted it while she was recovering from another bone graft operation, this one in the ABC Hospital in Mexico City and which required a year's recuperation. She no doubt used the easel her mother had erected over her bed so she could paint lying down. Kahlo painted a picture of herself in a wheelchair next to a portrait of Dr. Juan Farill, who did the bone graft. She is holding a painter's palette covered by a large heart. She often used the heart in her paintings as a sign of affection.

The surgeries were taking a toll on Kahlo's health, although around friends and visitors she still maintained her old cheerfulness. She did a lot of painting in those years of surgery and recuperation. *Still Life With Parrot,* done in 1951, shows a lush view of delicious-looking fruit, presided over by one of her pet parrots. Similar still-lifes were *Light (Fruit of Life)* and *Long Live Life,* both painted in 1954, the year of her death. They are full of color and the bursting promise of life. That same year, she painted herself in a deep-red shawl next to a portrait of Stalin. Her brush strokes were no longer as sure, but she continued working. Another self-portrait at that time shows a sketched image of a face on her forehead. In those later self-portraits, Kahlo began to decorate her forehead with symbols of thought.

In *Self-Portrait with Ixcuintle Dog and Sun,* she brings together the beloved elements of her life, Diego, a pet dog, herself as a young woman, and the land of Mexico, bathed in golden sunlight.

Preparations began in 1953 for Kahlo's first one-woman show in her native land. It would be a retrospective of her work at the National Institute of Fine Arts. But the planning dragged on, and Rivera began to wonder if she would live long enough to attend. A friend, Lola Alvarez Bravo, came to the rescue. She offered to show the paintings at her large Galeria de Arte Contemporaneo. Rivera made the arrangements, and Kahlo chipped in by making the invitations.

When the show opened in April 1953, it seemed doubtful that Kahlo would be able to attend. By then, she was bedridden and practically surviving on painkillers. But Frida wasn't dead yet. She arrived at the show in an ambulance with a police motorcycle escort, sirens wailing. Her canopied bed had been brought from her home and installed in the middle of the gallery. An informal receiving line was set up, and each guest came up to her bed to greet her. It was certainly a unique moment in the history of art.

Kahlo told a reporter from *Time* magazine, "I am not sick. I am broken. But I am happy to be alive as long as I can paint."

The next month, Kahlo was hospitalized again. This time doctors had to amputate her right leg below the knee because of a gangrenous condition. Kahlo spent three months in the hospital. Typical of her, she made light of her condition to visiting friends. In fact, she drew a picture of her severed leg in her diary and wrote these words, "*Pies para qué los quiero, si tengo alas pa' volar?*" (Feet, why do I want them if I have wings to fly?)

But Kahlo began to think seriously of suicide. "They have given me centuries of torture and at moments I almost lost my reason," she wrote in her diary in February 1954. "I keep on wanting to kill myself. Diego is what keeps me from it through my vain idea that he would miss me. He has told me that and I believe it. But never in my life have I suffered more. I will wait a while . . ."

But it's not certain that she was willing to wait. She was hospitalized in April and May, possibly after suicide attempts.

Even though she had left the Communist Party after her

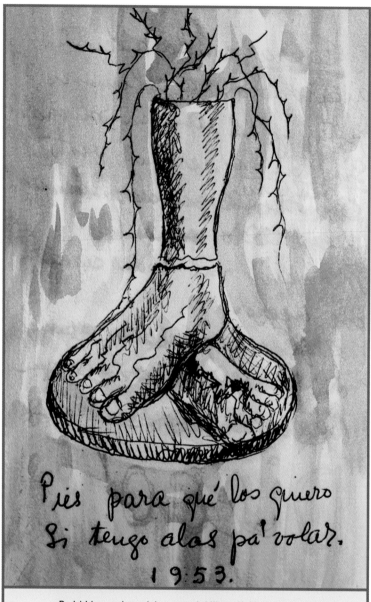

Pies para qué los quiero
Si tengo alas pa' volar.
1953.

Bedridden and surviving on painkillers, Kahlo had every reason to lose her characteristic vibrant spirit when doctors amputated her right leg in 1953. Instead, Kahlo refused to allow such an ordeal to get the best of her; a testament to her determination to enjoy life to the end, she drew a picture in her diary of her severed leg inscribed with the words, "Feet, why do I want them if I have wings to fly?"

husband had been expelled, Kahlo rejoined the party in 1952. She renounced her Trotskyite beliefs and embraced Stalin. Stalin, who governed the Soviet Union with an iron fist for 30 years, died the following year, but not before he ordered the execution of 19 Jewish activists for an imagined "Zionist conspiracy." (Zionism was the movement that inspired Jews to return to their homeland in Israel.)

As part of her new dedication to Communism, Kahlo painted *Marxism Will Give Health to the Sick* in 1954. She left behind an unfinished portrait of Stalin. By then, Frida was clearly dying. But she had to make one more political statement.

Long Live Life!

Kahlo's final days were a mixture of sweetness, anger, and nastiness. As a former nurse, Judith Ferreto, put it: "During those days, she was going down rapidly." Ferreto added, "I think that she foresaw that she was going down and down. . . ."

Kahlo and Ferreto had a fight one day during a visit by Ferreto. Kahlo thought the nurse was bossing her around in her own home. She was very touchy and irritable at times. For instance, she no longer wanted children to visit, even though she had loved her nieces. "After the amputation, she hated children," Ferreto said. "The operation destroyed a personality. She loved life, she really loved life, but it was completely different after they amputated her leg."

Rivera himself was upset by Kahlo's behavior. Raquel Tibol, an art critic and longtime friend, recalled that once, when Frida was very sick and lay in a drugged state upstairs, Rivera arrived at the house and tried to eat lunch.

"He had come home to eat, but he didn't want to eat," Tibol said.

Kahlo and Rivera pose on the patio of the Casa Azul. Despite her weak condition, Kahlo insisted on inviting a hundred guests to the house in Coyoacán to celebrate her 47th birthday on July 6, 1954. Kahlo would die just seven days later.

"He began to cry like a child, and he said, 'If I were brave, I would kill her. I cannot stand to see her suffer so.' He cried like a child, cried and cried."

On another occasion, Kahlo threw a bottle of water at Rivera. He managed to duck out of the way. The sound of the breaking glass took the anger out of her. "Why did I do it?" she asked, crying. "Tell me, why did I do it? If I continue like this, I would prefer to die."

At other times, when Rivera had been away working and returned, Kahlo would say, "My child, where have you been, my child?" in a soft, loving voice.

Kahlo became a serious drug addict and got Rivera and others to buy her drugs. Once she asked another friend to give her an injection. He asked where he was going to get the drug, and she pointed to a drawer in a bureau. He opened it and found "a box with thousands of vials of Demerol."

Oddly, at the end of June 1954, Kahlo's health seemed to improve. She began talking about plans for the future, even saying she wanted to adopt a child. She had been invited to the Soviet Union, but said she wouldn't go without Rivera. He had been ousted from the Communist Party and had not been readmitted even though he had asked to be.

Kahlo was looking forward to the silver wedding anniversary with Rivera on August 21. She planned a "great Mexican fiesta" and urged her friends to bring lots of people.

Meanwhile, on July 2, she disobeyed her doctors and left her bed to join an anti-American demonstration organized by the Communist Party in Mexico City. The event was to protest the removal of Guatemala's liberal president Jacobo Arbenz and the suspected involvement of the American Central Intelligence Agency (CIA) in replacing him with the reactionary General Castillo Armas. About 10,000 people showed up, and Kahlo was the star of the show. Rivera pushed her in her wheelchair through the crowds, and people fell in line behind them. Photographs show her looking wan and weak, but bravely holding a banner in one hand and making a fist with the other. She had covered her head with a kerchief and she was not her usual jaunty self, but the rings on the fingers of her clenched fist glittered in the light of that gray, rainy day. Kahlo sat in her wheelchair for four hours, joining in the cry, "*Gringos asesinos, fuera!*" (Yankee assassins, get out!). She had been suffering with pneumonia, and being out in that damp weather for so long took a toll on her.

LAST BIRTHDAY PARTY

July 6 was Frida's 47th birthday. She insisted on a celebration, and her friends gathered in the Casa Azul for the party. It was to be her last.

A hundred people came for her birthday celebration. She got dressed and made up her face. She was carried downstairs to the dining room where she greeted her friends. They ate a lunch of Mexican delicacies, and Kahlo seemed cheerful. Later, she was carried back upstairs and placed in her bed. She continued to talk to friends until late at night. She was not afraid of death. However, she had a dread of lying in her coffin and being lowered into the ground. It was in that position that she had suffered so much in her life. So, the decision was made that she would be cremated.

The last pages of her diary contain drawings of skeletons in costumes and strange winged female creatures. She wrote, "*Muertes en relajo*" (the dead having a fling). "We look for calm or 'peace,' because we anticipate death, since we die every moment," she wrote. The final drawing is of a dark angel rising into the sky. Accompanying it are the words, "*Espero alegre la salida—y espero no volver jamas. Frida.*" (I hope for a happy exit and I hope never to come back.)

When Kahlo's old school chum and lawyer, Manuel Gonzalez Ramirez, visited her, he said they talked openly about her death, "because Frida was not afraid of it."

The day before she died, she told her nurse that she felt better. She said she had no pain. Rivera visited her in the afternoon, and she started giving him advice. Frida warned him, "If you want your life to be aimless as a kite, just blown about by the wind, then that's the way it would be." Rivera told the nurse he would give her sleeping pills. "Frida usually put a bunch in her mouth all at once," nurse Mayet said. "She was supposed to take only seven, so I told Señor Diego that, and I counted the pills that were in the jar."

Frida gave Rivera a ring she had hidden away as an anniversary present. Rivera said he asked Frida why she was giving him the ring so early, and she replied, "Because I feel I am going to leave you very soon."

"I sat beside her bed until 2:30 in the morning," Rivera said. Then he left her to go to his San Angel studio. When he returned in the morning, the nurse told him of the pain Frida had suffered in the night: "At four o'clock she complained of severe discomfort. When a doctor arrived at daybreak, he found that she had died a short time before of an embolism (clot) of the lungs."

"When I went into her room to look at her," Rivera wrote, "her face was tranquil and seemed more beautiful than ever."

Mayet said she counted the sleeping pills and found that 11 were gone. Had Frida deliberately taken an overdose? Had she taken them accidentally? There was considerable speculation about the cause of her death. But her doctor, Velasco y Polo, insisted the cause was the embolism.

As for Rivera, those present said he turned old immediately. He locked himself in the bedroom and refused to see anyone as crowds of friends arrived at the Casa Azul. Later, he told his assistant Emmy Lou Packard, "I had no idea I was going to miss her so much."

It was July 13, 1954. Rain was falling, wetting the beautiful garden of the Casa Azul that Frida loved so much and would never see again.

THE RIGHT ARTIST FOR THE RIGHT TIME

It almost seemed that Frida Kahlo's spirit was reluctant to leave her body. When a friend, Olga Campos, bent down to kiss her, she screamed when she thought she saw Frida's skin react with goosebumps. Then Rivera claimed he saw her hair stand on end and called the doctor.

"We're not entirely sure that she's really dead," he said. But he was convinced when the doctor opened a vein and no blood flowed.

When Frida's body was being wheeled into the flames at the crematorium, it suddenly sat upright. Her hair, in flames, glowed

The hammer and sickle emblem of the Communist party is draped over Frida Kahlo's casket at the Mexican Palace of Fine Arts where more than 600 mourners came to pay their last respects. The placement of the Communist flag caused a scandal at the funeral when Rivera refused to have it removed. Although Rivera compounded Kahlo's physical wounds with emotional ones throughout their life together, after her death he wrote in his autobiography, "the most wonderful part of my life had been my love for Frida."

like a wreath around her head. Witnesses screamed. But then the body fell back down and was consumed by the flames. To some, it seemed that Kahlo's spirit was still strong enough, even in death, to make a final statement in favor of life. After all, her last painting, a still-life, carried the inscription, "*Viva la vida!*" (Long live life!).

More than 600 people came to mourn Kahlo's death. Among the honor guard was former Mexican president Lazaro Cardenas. The mourners walked solemnly in the rain behind the hearse carrying her body, which was dressed in her favorite Tehuana costume and bedecked with her spectacular jewelry, to the Palace of Fine Arts. There, Frida Kahlo lay in state while mourners passed her coffin.

Something of a scandal erupted when a former art student, Arturo Garcia Bustos, draped a Communist flag with hammer and sickle over her coffin. Andres Iduarte, who had known Frida in her school days and was now director of the Palace of Fine Arts, had asked Rivera not to turn the funeral into a political demonstration. Rivera had agreed, but he refused to have the flag removed. Iduarte was later fired over the incident.

The body was driven slowly through the gray drizzle along the Avenida Juarez to the Pantheon Civil de Delores, the municipal cemetery, for cremation. Her friends and family sang hymns and her favorite Mexican songs as the fire consumed the earthly remains of one of Mexico's most treasured artists.

Rivera gathered Kahlo's ashes in a red silk scarf and placed them in a cedar box. He took them to the Casa Azul in Coyoacán, where they are on display today in a pre-Columbian urn. Despite all the pain he had given Kahlo, Rivera was genuinely devastated by her death. He looked pale and drawn at the funeral and never really regained his old flash. One consolation was that he was readmitted to the Communist Party as a reward for refusing to have the hammer-and-sickle flag removed from Frida's coffin.

"The most tragic day of my life was 13 July 1954," he wrote in his autobiography. "I had lost my beloved Frida forever. Too late now, I realized that the most wonderful part of my life had been my love for Frida." He later told a friend, "Numerous critics in various countries have characterized Frida Kahlo's work as being the most vigorously rooted in Mexican folk art of all the Moderns. That's what I think, too." He added that her work "represents one of the most powerful and truthful human documents of our times. It will

Today, visitors can visit Kahlo's home in Coyoacán to develop a more personal under-standing of the fascinating artist. Particularly of interest to museum visitors is the studio that Rivera designed and built for Kahlo in 1946. On her easel is a portrait of the Marxist leader, Josef Stalin, which was left unfinished at the time of her death.

be of inestimable value for future generations."

Kahlo's home is open to visitors today. Rivera gave it to the Mexican people in 1955, and it was formally opened in 1958. The tall windows facing the street are still bricked in, the security measure to protect Trotsky when he lived there. The grotesque Judas figures that Frida liked guard the door. The house also contains many of her own paintings, as well as paintings by Rivera and others that she had purchased over the years. The rest of the house remains as it was in her lifetime, still cluttered with her photos, dolls, toys, and the other souvenirs with which she liked to surround herself. In her upstairs studio is an unfinished portrait of Josef Stalin. From the hallway through an open door is a view of her cherished garden.

On the first anniversary of Kahlo's death, Rivera painted a smiling portrait of her with the inscription, "For the star of my eyes, Fridita, who is still mine, 13 July 1955, Diego." Later that month, on July 29, Rivera married the publisher Emma Hurtado. But his new wife, as charming and beautiful as she was, was certainly no Frida Kahlo. It's unlikely that Rivera ever recovered from the death of the woman he had treated so insensitively for so many years.

Shortly after his marriage to Hurtado, Rivera went to the Soviet Union for cobalt treatments for prostate cancer. He continued to paint, both in Moscow and back in Mexico. Three

FRIDA KAHLO TODAY

Often grouped in with her husband Diego Rivera as a member of the Mexican Renaissance, interest in Frida Kahlo has seen a rebirth as well. In fact, Kahlo's name was virtually only known to the most educated members of the art world when the first biography dedicated to the artist was published in 1983 by Hayden Herrera. Since 2000, however, there has been a proliferation of books and exhibitions pertaining to the artist's work. A novel based on Kahlo's life, Kate Braverman's *The Incantation of Frida K.* (Seven Stories), and Jonah Winter's children's book *Frida* (Scholastic), were both published in 2002, two unprecedented ways of communicating Frida Kahlo's story. Probably the most intriguing profile of Kahlo's life is Miramax's motion picture *Frida*, which was released in October 2002. Although Frida Kahlo lived the majority of her life behind her husband Diego Rivera's immense shadow, she has truly eclipsed him, capturing the imagination of story-tellers everywhere.

years after Frida Kahlo's death, Rivera died of a heart attack in his San Angel studio on November 24, 1957.

In February 2002, a large exhibition at Washington's National Museum of Women in the Arts featured Kahlo's paintings, along with those of Georgia O'Keeffe and Emily Carr. More than 28,000 people attended, and it was believed that Kahlo's works were the major attraction. Visitors left with totebags full of Frida memorabilia, her unsmiling image on everything from watches to computer mouse pads.

As Gregorio Luke, director of the Museum of Latin American Art in California, said of Kahlo's recent popularity: "Frida Kahlo has been the right artist for the right time."

Chronology

1907   Born Magdalena Carmen Frida Kahlo Calderón on July 6 in the Casa Azul in Coyoacán, Mexico, the third of Matilde Calderón and Guillermo Kahlo's four daughters.

1910   The Mexican Revolution begins. Kahlo will claim to be born during this year so that the year of her birth will coincide with the birth of the revolution.

1913   Contracts polio, permanently affecting her right leg.

1922   Enters the National Preparatory School, becomes member of mischief-making Cachuchas; teases Diego Rivera, who is painting a mural, *Creation,* at the school. Tells schoolmates she wants to have his baby.

1925   Permanently injured in a streetcar accident in Mexico City.

1925   Begins painting, using easel and mirror set up over her bed by her mother.

1927   Meets Diego Rivera again; asks him to look at her paintings.

1929   Marries Rivera on August 21.

1930   Goes to San Francisco, where Rivera has commissions to paint two murals. She is hospitalized with a problem with her foot.

1932   Goes with Rivera to Detroit, where Rivera has commissions to paint murals. Frida is hospitalized for a miscarriage. Her mother dies.

1933   Returns with Rivera to New York, where Rivera is commissioned by Nelson Rockefeller to paint a mural at the RCA Building.

1934   Back in Mexico, the married couple lives in a double house linked by a bridge in San Angel. Rivera begins an affair with Frida's younger sister, Cristina.

1935 Moves out of the house and takes an apartment, travels to New York with friends, returns, and reconciles with Rivera.

1937 Leon Trotsky and his wife arrive in Mexico and live in Casa Azul in hiding. Kahlo begins an affair with Trotsky.

1938 Edward G. Robinson buys four of Kahlo's paintings; her first one-person exhibit runs at the Julien Levy Gallery in New York.

1939 The Louvre buys painting, *The Frame*. Divorces Rivera.

1940 *The Two Fridas* and *The Wounded Table* are included in the International Surrealism Exhibition at the Gallery of Mexican Art. Leon Trotsky is murdered by an agent of Josef Stalin. Frida and Rivera remarry.

1941 Father dies; Kahlo moves to the Casa Azul in Coyoacán.

1942 *Self-Portrait with Braid* shown at the Museum of Modern Art's *Twentieth-Century Portraits*.

1943 Paintings are exhibited at a group show, *A Century of the Portrait in Mexico (1830-1942)* at the Benjamin Franklin Library, Mexico City; in *Mexican Art Today* at the Philadelphia Museum of Art, and at Peggy Guggenheim's Art of This Century Gallery in New York.

1943 Begins teaching at the Ministry of Public Education's School of Painting and Sculpture, La Esmeralda.

1946 Surgery performed on Kahlo's spine.

1947 *Self-Portrait as a Tehuana (Diego in My Thoughts)* exhibited in *Forty-Five Self-Portraits by Mexican Painters from XVIII to the XX Centuries* at the National Institute of Fine Arts in Mexico City.

1949 *The Love Embrace of the Universe, the Earth (Mexico), Me, Diego and Mr. Xolotl,* is exhibited at the inaugural exhibition of the Salon de la Plastica Mexicana.

1950 Hospitalized for nine months for recurring spinal problems.

1953 Frida's only individual exhibition in Mexico is held at the Galeria de Arte Contemporaneo. She attends, although she has to greet guests lying in bed in the gallery.

1954 Critically ill with bronchial pneumonia, but takes part in an anti-American demonstration over Guatemala on July 2. Dies on July 13.

1957 Diego Rivera dies.

1958 The Casa Azul is opened to the public as the Frida Kahlo Museum.

1983 The first full-length biography of Kahlo, written by Hayden Herrera, is published.

2002 The major motion picture *Frida* and several books on Kahlo's life and art are released.

Bibliography

Alcantara, Isabel and Egnoff, Sandra. *Frida Kahlo and Diego Rivera.* Munich, London, New York: Prestel Verlag, 1999.

Cockroft, James. *Diego Rivera.* Philadelphia: Chelsea House Publishers, 1991.

Hardin, Terri. *Frida Kahlo: A Modern Master.* New York: Smithmark Publishers, 1997.

Herrera, Hayden. *Frida: A Biography of Frida Kahlo.* New York: Harper & Row, 1983.

Kettenmann, Andrea. *Kahlo.* Köln, Germany: Taschen, 2000.

Moore Thomas. *The Soul's Religion.* New York: HarperCollins, 2002.

Zamora, Martha. *Frida Kahlo: The Brush of Anguish.* San Francisco: Chronicle Books, 1990.

Websites

The Art History Network: Frida Kahlo
   http://www.arthistory.net/artists/kahlo.html

Biography of Frida Kahlo (Keyword: Kahlo)
   http://www.brain-juice.com

Frida Kahlo and Contemporary Thoughts
   http://www.fridakahlo.it

Frida Kahlo: Diego's Lover and Friend
   http://www.fbuch.com/fridakahlo.htm

Frida Kahlo in the Florence Arquin Papers
   http://www.archivesofamericanart.si.edu/htgmonth/hispanic/arquin.htm

Further Reading

Casagrande, Louis B. and S.A. Johnson. *Focus on Mexico: Modern Life in an Ancient Land.* New York: Lerner, 1986.

Fisher, Leonard E. *Pyramid of the Sun, Pyramid of the Moon.* New York: Macmillan, 1988.

Herrera, Hayden. *Frida Kahlo: The Paintings.* New York: HarperCollins, 1991.

Kahlo, Frida. *The Diary of Frida Kahlo: An Intimate Self-Portrait.* New York: Abradale Press, 2002.

Kettenmann, Andrea. *Frida Kahlo: Pain and Passion.* New York: Taschen America, 2000.

Stein, R. Conrad. *Mexico.* New York: Children's Press, 1984.

Winter, Jonah and Ana Juan. *Frida.* New York: Scholastic Press, 2002.

Index

Picture Credits

About the Author

John Morrison is a longtime Philadelphia newspaperman who has worked as a reporter, writer, and editor. He has had short stories and poetry published and has edited several novels for a Dell Publishing subsidiary.